TALES FROM THE
OAKLAND RAIDERS
SIDELINE

A COLLECTION OF THE GREATEST
RAIDERS STORIES EVER TOLD

TOM FLORES
WITH MATT FULKS

FOREWORD BY
JIM PLUNKETT

SPORTS
PUBLISHING

Sports Publishing books may be purchased in bulk at special discounts for sales promotion, corporate gifts, fund-raising, or educational purposes. Special editions can also be created to specifications. For details, contact the Special Sales Department, Sports Publishing, 307 West 36th Street, 11th Floor, New York, NY 10018 or sportspubbooks@skyhorsepublishing.com.

Sports Publishing® is a registered trademark of Skyhorse Publishing, Inc.®, a Delaware corporation.

Visit our website at www.sportspubbooks.com.

10 9 8 7 6 5 4 3 2 1

Library of Congress Cataloging-in-Publication Data is available on file.

Cover design by Tom Lau
Cover photo credit AP Photos

ISBN: 978-1-68358-139-0
Ebook ISBN: 978-1-68358-156-7

Printed in the United States of America

This book is dedicated to all the past and present warriors who have worn or are wearing the Silver and Black. In particular, we remember the great Raiders who are no longer with us, including: Lyle Alzado, John Matuszak, Dave Dalby, Hewritt Dixon, Neal Colzie, Duke O'Steen, Eddie Erdelatz, and three of the original owners—Chet Soda, Ed McGraw, and Wayne Valley. You will always be remembered, and your legacies live on.

CONTENTS

PREFACE

RESURGING RAIDERS

When this book was first written, the stories were intended to stand on their own. Upon reviewing them for this re-release, we think that they do. Nevertheless, Tom wanted to share his thoughts in a new first chapter about some of the Raider greats who have passed away since 2003, about former coach Jon Gruden, and about the current state of the organization. He wanted to lead off this updated version where he led off the 2012 update, with the biggest loss in the organization's history, former coach, general manager, and owner Al Davis, who passed away on October 8, 2011. He was 82.

It seems appropriate to start this update with the passing of Al Davis because his death is one of the most monumental events in the history of the Raiders' organization. After all, he *was* the Raiders. He was, without question, one of the best micromanagers I've ever been around. No one made a move—whether it was signing a player or changing the brand of paper in the front office—without his approval. But no one loved the Raiders more than Al Davis did. There'll never be another like him.

We all knew he was in failing health but it was hard to imagine that he would pass away. Come on, he's Al Davis! That weekend was extremely sad for those of us who knew him, but the team responded with a miracle win on Sunday.

The day after Al's passing, the Raiders were facing the Texans in Houston. Looking at the stats from the game, we shouldn't have won that day. The Texans had nearly 500 yards of offense (473) and held the Raiders to 278. On top of that, the Raiders had only 94 yards of rushing and 11 first downs. No, statistically we maybe shouldn't have won.

As we all know, though—and what Al always stressed—it comes down to the players on the field making the plays. That was the case on that Sunday.

With the Raiders leading 25-20 and less than a minute left, the Texans were driving. Their quarterback, Matt Schaub, had Houston at the Raiders 5-yard line with seven seconds left. On the game's final play, Schaub threw a soft pass to Jacoby Jones in the end zone. Wouldn't you know it, there was Michael Huff to pick it off and preserve the Raiders win.

The Raiders finished the 2011 season with a record of 8-8, but Al Davis' shadow was around for the rest of the season. It likely will be for years to come.

Unfortunately, some of the young guys—especially those who have been with the organization since 2010 or so—didn't get to know the Al Davis that others of us did.

They won't know the man who was fiercely loyal to his friends but demanded your commitment. He demanded that you love the game as much as he did. I don't know that anyone could love it as much as he did but he needed to believe that you did. That's how John Madden survived coaching for him, and that's how I survived as a player, assistant coach, head coach, and broadcaster. Don't get me wrong: he'd still chew me out if I said something during a broadcast that he didn't like. I was more diplomatic than he was. He was the villain, a role he enjoyed playing to its fullest. There were times that he wanted me to be more critical and tougher on the guys.

Although he was a hands-on owner, he wasn't as directly involved during the game as people thought he was. The perception was that he was pulling the strings during games because he had a phone next to him that was visible when they showed him on TV. But he never messed with his coaches during the game. Most of his phone calls were to check on injuries. Personally, I never talked to him when I was on the sidelines. That's not to say he didn't occasionally send down suggestions. From time to time, feeling he needed to be part of the action, he'd send messages down to the coaches on the field. I never delivered those when I was an assistant. Somewhere I have an envelope full of messages he sent.

In my opinion, the game of football is better because he was a part of it for so many years. The story was told in newspaper articles when he passed away but people don't realize how instrumental he was during the AFL-NFL merger. It's generally thought that Lamar Hunt of the Chiefs and Tex Schramm of the Cowboys were the two main people who put the merger together. As commissioner of the AFL at the time, Al somehow persuaded Baltimore, Cleveland, and Pittsburgh to move to the AFL from the NFL. When that happened, the merger came together.

His shadow is still with the Raiders and will continue to be. A flame is lit in the corner of the stadium prior to every home game. The initial one, a little more than a week after his passing, was lit, appropriately, by John Madden. That day, every generation of Raiders was represented on the field. It was quite an emotional event.

If you're wondering how former players and staff felt about Al Davis, consider this. During his birthday weekend, on the Fourth of July in 2012, when he would've turned 83, we had a private celebration in Las Vegas hosted by the Davis family. There were 280 people in attendance, including players, coaches, personnel, and their spouses. It was a great celebration of a man who meant so much to all of us.

Right around the time of that celebration, we lost another great Raider, Ben Davidson, to cancer. Ben was such a neat guy. In the days leading up to our trip to Vegas, he asked his wife Kathy to call and tell everyone that he couldn't make the trip. As soon as we arrived at the hotel we learned that he'd passed away. I knew Ben wouldn't survive this round of cancer too long. The last time I saw him was in April 2012 at a golf tournament. We were chatting and he said he had to go back home for more treatment. Damn cancer! But if you asked Ben to do something, he never turned you down. He showed up for all of the events I hosted.

Without question, Ben Davidson was one of the true icons and great characters in the history of the NFL.

Of course, since this book was written in 2003, we've lost other great Raiders including George Blanda (September 2010), Jack Tatum (July 2010), and Gene Upshaw (August 2008). Each one was a great Raider. Blanda, it seemed, wore an "S" on his chest. He was a little older than Al, but he played until 1975. Jack was one of the most intimidating players I've ever seen with the way he played the game, but we could be having a team meeting in a room with a few guys and Jack was so quiet that we wouldn't know he was there. As for Gene, who took some heat when he led the Player's Association, he played for only the Raiders. That's very unique. Few guys in the NFL through the 1970s can say that.

Even though this is a Raiders book, I do need to mention the death of two more individuals who were important to me, Lamar Hunt and Hank Stram. There is more about each of these men later in the book, but I need to reiterate what I said there.

Toward the end of my playing career, in 1969, Hank gave me a chance with the Chiefs after Buffalo had cut me. I spent part of a season with the Chiefs and won a Super Bowl with them.

Hank was a very innovative football man. As a head coach, you take something away from all of the coaches who have influenced your career. That held true for me, especially with Hank Stram.

As far as Lamar Hunt, all I can say is that he was one of the best owners ever in the history of the NFL.

Preface

KENNY "THE SNAKE" STABLER

Damn cancer took another NFL icon and Raiders great, Kenny "The Snake" Stabler. In fact, since the last edition of this book, two big things happened with Snake: he was inducted into the Pro Football Hall of Fame and he lost a battle with colon cancer. Unfortunately, the two events didn't happen in that order.

The Snake died of colon cancer on July 8, 2015. About a month later, the Pro Football Hall of Fame announced that he was one of two senior nominees for induction. And, sure enough, that led to his induction in 2016. But that was such a travesty. Snake's contemporaries and long-time NFL reporters asked the same question for years: When is Kenny Stabler going to be inducted into the Hall of Fame? He should've been inducted long before 2016.

Had Snake played in New York, for instance, he would've been in the Hall of Fame years earlier. The comparison I like to make is Snake to Joe Namath, who was inducted in 1985. What didn't Snake do that Namath did? Although Snake played two more years, their career numbers are very close. Snake threw for 27,938 yards; Namath threw for 27,663. Stabler threw for 194 touchdowns and 222 interceptions, compared to 173 and 220 for Namath. They each won a Super Bowl.

Maybe the question shouldn't be, "What didn't Snake do that Namath did," but rather, "What didn't Namath do that Stabler did?" Namath was a two-time AFL MVP, although he never won the award after the AFL-NFL merger, he was an All-Pro one time, went to one Pro Bowl, and won one AFL championship (Namath didn't win an AFC championship). Snake, on the other hand, won the NFL MVP award once, was a two-time All-Pro, went to four Pro Bowls, and played in five AFC championship games. And, if you're into passer ratings, Stabler's was higher at 75.3 to Namath's 65.5.

Both guys were charismatic and had a smile on their faces all the time. The biggest difference? One played in New York City and the other played in Oakland.

Snake was wonderful to be around, on and off the field, to everybody around him. In the huddle, he was all business. He wasn't a yeller or screamer, but you could look into his eyes and see his intensity. Players around him knew when he was on a tear which gave them so much more confidence.

When I was an assistant coach under John Madden, if Snake was having a bad day in practice, John would say that Snake will work his way out of it. So we generally let him go on his own and work it out. More often than not, though, he completed almost every pass he threw in practice. He became competitive against our guys with fire coming out of his ears and snot coming out of his nose. Even in practice he was like a bull coming out at the rodeo. There's a lot to the old saying, "The way you practice is the way you play." The way Snake performed on Sunday was a reflection of how hard he worked in practice during that week.

It was a shock when we found out that he died. No one knew he had colon cancer. He didn't want anyone to know. His long-time girlfriend, Kim Bush, called me when he passed away. She said, "I know Kenny would've wanted me to call you and explain." That's how we found out. He didn't want any sympathy, and he was proud of his private life. It was typical of the Snake.

"CHUCKIE"

Looking at the team's "recent" history, there's one person that we didn't address in the first book, whom I've come to appreciate a great deal over the years: Jon Gruden. In 2000, Jon led the Raiders to a 12-4 record, the team's first division title since 1990, and, eventually, the AFC championship. The next year, the Raiders won the AFC West but lost to New England in the playoffs in the "Tuck Rule" game. At the end of the next season, under coach Bill Callahan, the Raiders reached Super Bowl XXXVII against Tampa Bay, which at the time was coached by Jon. That game, which Tampa Bay won 48-21, was over in the first quarter. The Raiders had Jerry Rice and Timmy Brown, but Tampa charged down the field and the Raiders couldn't come back.

Jon was an intense guy on and off the field with his "Chuckie" look all of the time. He was fun to watch because he was so intense. He was vocally active in practice and in the game, much like he is now as a TV analyst. I saw him during at Raiders training camp in 2012, and even with that scowl on his face and excited intensity in his voice, he said, "Is this great or what!" He loved the Raiders. That type of coach is infectious. He is a force. He got this organization back to winning. You have to stay on guys all of the time, but Jon did it his way.

When he became the coach of the Raiders, he was a young guy, which is what Al had wanted. I think that's largely what he saw in Lane Kiffin, although that didn't work out as well for the organization. Al figured he could mold young coaches into what he wanted. Jon had the tenacity and fire and spirit that Al loved.

Jon always had affection for the Raiders, and he still has it today. He's always shown a passion and a love for the Silver and Black.

A RAIDER RESURGENCE

After the death of Al Davis, his son, Mark, took over. Mark loves the Raiders. He was a little pain in the ass at training camp as a kid, but he grew up with the organization. He gets very emotional during the course of a game. But he's not his dad. No one is. With Mark at the helm and Al no longer with us, the personality of the organization has changed because Al isn't the driving force. From 1963 until his death, Al was the Raiders, seven days a week, 365 days of the year. He set the standard for the legacy.

You can't reshape the legacy; we don't want to reshape it. Toward the end of Al's life and during the transition to Mark, the Raiders fell on some dark times. After going to the Super Bowl at the end of the 2002 season, things went from bad to worse. The team did not have a winning record from 2003 until the 2016 season. (They were 8-8 in 2010 and 2011.) But what a resurgence 2016 was! The Raiders went 12-4, which was tied for the second-best record in the AFC.

The type of turnaround we've seen is the type that can only start at the top. Mark has demonstrated an understanding that it is important to seek advice from others who have been around the game, people such as Ron Wolf, Ken Herock, John Madden, and, I'd like to think, me. We are family.

If the Raiders get back to consistent winning, they'll still be the Raiders. If they win, the history will continue to be strong. If they don't win, over time the history will be, well, just history. That could be said of a lot of franchises. It's similar to George Steinbrenner and his sons with the New York Yankees. Lamar Hunt will always be the Chiefs, even with his son, Clark, in there as owner. The Raiders will always be Al Davis, but we'll see over time if they also take on the personality of Mark Davis.

When Mark made the trade for Carson Palmer in 2011, he took some heat for it. We talked before he made the trade. I told him then and I'd say it again today: "Don't do it if you don't feel it's right, but don't second guess yourself afterwards. If you go with it, deal with it and don't look back."

Mark knows he doesn't have all of the same abilities Al had and recognizes the importance of getting someone in there who could offer assistance. That's where Reggie McKenzie came in. Following the 2012 season, Mark hired Reggie as the team's general manager. We drafted Reggie as a linebacker in the tenth round out of Tennessee in 1985, and he played for me for three seasons. He was a good, tough linebacker. In fact, his strength as a player was his toughness. He was a solid player; very intelligent on and off the field.

His twin brother Raleigh played for Washington and is now a scout with the Raiders. Since his playing career, he's become a knowledgeable football mind with a strong nose for talent.

When Reggie started scouting in 1994, Ron hired him and took him to Green Bay. Reggie got incredible guidance under Ron, who told me once that Reggie's biggest strength was his ability to spot talent. We've seen that play out in how he's built the Raiders through the draft and free agent signings. After the 2015 season, the Raiders had six Pro Bowl selections, five of whom were drafted or signed on Reggie's watch.

One key in building the type of organization Reggie's building isn't only player acquisition but also being the type of leader who develops an atmosphere where people want to work. Reggie, as well as Raleigh, are both quality guys. Reggie is very positive in the way he approaches everything, and he knows how to go about his business without puffing out his chest.

Almost three years to the day of Reggie being hired, he hired Jack Del Rio as the team's new head coach. I remember Jack as a great high school star in Hayward, California, which is down the block from the Coliseum. Jack was a good fit. I didn't know him personally, but I always liked him as a player and he'd been a good, fiery head coach with Jacksonville for nearly a decade.

The combination of Reggie and Jack is very good for the franchise. When Reggie joined us as a player, we were a good team. He'd grown up watching us in our heyday, and he remembered all of that when he became the GM. When Jack joined the organization, he realized it wasn't the same culture that we were known for under Al Davis, and he wanted to get it back.

For 19 pretty good years, the organization had John Madden and me, and we knew how to work with Al. The culture of professional football is different now, but having Reggie and Jack on the same page can mean only good things for the organization. You have to have a system, and you have to have people who know how to run that system.

2014 DRAFT: GETTING A MACK TRUCK
AND A HIGH-PERFORMANCE CARR

When Reggie McKenzie came in, the organization was a mess after several poor free agent signings and draft picks that didn't work out. Besides spotting talent, Reggie is great at understanding character, which is a huge component for Reggie. Mind you, football character is different from church character. In football, character guys are the ones who'll do their best to stay out of trouble off the field but also guys who just want to be here and play, as opposed to players who out there for the paycheck or the adulation. Reggie's developed a squad full of those character guys in a short amount of time.

Two of them came during the 2014 NFL Draft. Going into that draft, in need of a franchise quarterback, the Raiders were picking fifth overall. Derek Carr, out of Fresno State, was Reggie's top-rated quarterback in the draft that included Johnny Manziel.

This was a strange draft, though. Before Manziel dropped lower than most people expected (22nd overall), another player dropped lower than Reggie expected, when linebacker Khalil Mack was available when the Raiders picked fifth. For a moment I'm sure it was a tough decision for Reggie, but when you can get a player who is dominating, the type of defensive player a quarterback looks for as soon as he comes to the line of scrimmage, you have to take him.

So with their first-round selection, the Raiders took Mack out of Buffalo. It was a great decision. Khalil does damage, whether he's one-on-one or two-on-one. And he's a quiet leader who goes hard on every play.

With that pick, obviously that left Derek open. Only two other quarterbacks were taken that first day: Manziel by the Browns and Teddy Bridgewater by the Vikings on the last pick of the first round. When Derek made it through the first day, I knew it'd be a restless night for Reggie, hoping and praying that Derek would be there when Oakland picked fourth in the second round. When he arrived that morning, Reggie had a big smile on his face. I think he really felt he was going to get Derek. Sure enough, Houston, Dallas, and Cleveland all picked linemen, and the Raiders got Derek with the 36th overall pick.

As we saw in 2016, Derek is a quarterback around which a franchise can build. He was one of the missing links for this franchise. The quarterback situation is part of the reason this organization fell on hard times. Teams rarely can miss on a quarterback and still be successful. You can miss on a running back or a lineman, but you have only one quarterback. If you miss on him, it can cost the organization years.

Just look what happened with JaMarcus Russell. He was the first player selected in the 2007 NFL Draft, signed for $36 million, and turned out to be one of the biggest busts in not only Raiders' history, but NFL history. The Raiders have never had a big war chest of cash, so that set the organization back three years.

There's no telling what will happen with Derek, but as we write this, he's a great fit and not someone who's likely going to affect the organization negatively. He is a player who has an angelic face with fire in his eyes when he competes. One of his best qualities is a short memory. If something bad happens, he doesn't make excuses or dwell on it; he just gets ready for the next chance. On top of that, he has the mindset that he can make plays in the fourth quarter. Sometimes that can be a detriment because quarterbacks tend to believe they can make plays that are nearly impossible, but Derek's not going to leave anything on the table. He's going to give his all and make the plays.

I like to watch quarterbacks when they're not involved in the play, once they're not handling the ball. I like to watch their body language. Some guys are quiet and some are in a different world. Derek's always active and proactive. He's congratulating other guys. Not in a cheerleader way, but in a leader kind of way.

On Christmas Eve 2016, Santa left a big chunk of coal in the Raiders' stockings when Derek was sacked in the fourth quarter against Indianapolis and broke his fibula. The wind was knocked out of Raider Nation, from the field to the press box. We won that game, but Derek was so valuable to the team that there was an empty feeling going into the AFC Wild Card game a couple weeks later against Houston. What seemed like the makings of a remarkable season ended in a thud.

What we've seen out of Derek, though, is that he's proved himself as a young quarterback who's a team guy and their offensive leader. He's a great ambassador for the Raiders and gives us a reason to be excited about the future.

LEAVING OUR ROOTS FOR THE STRIP

Raiders owner Mark Davis announced during the writing of this update that the Raiders are moving to Las Vegas. To me, this is different than when Al Davis decided to move the team to Los Angeles in the early 1980s. When we went to Los Angeles, we had an instant place to play in the Coliseum. The crowd was different—more laid back—but the fans knew us well and we knew the area well. Going to Vegas is completely different, including the city building the team a venue unlike any other in the NFL.

Las Vegas Stadium, as it's being called now and is scheduled to open in 2020, will be at one end of the Las Vegas Strip. It's supposed to have retractable doors and a glass-domed roof. There's supposed to be a monstrous video board on the outside, an eternal flame in memory of Al and hold 65,000 people. The price tag is estimated to be a little under $2 billion.

The need to leave Oakland–Alameda County Coliseum is necessary but the timing is somewhat unfortunate. In 2016, with the team playing better, the stadium was rocking again. The Silver-and-Black faithful were going crazy. The problem, though, is that the stadium is more than 50 years old, and it is in need of repairs and upgrades. As great as it was to see it rocking again, I don't know that we want it rocking too much. But Raider fans are passionate and make Oakland–Alameda an intimidating place to play. With a move to Las Vegas, we won't recapture the "Black Hole," the great tailgate parties, and the other nuances that make the Oakland Raiders famous. It's not likely to happen in Vegas because it could be a different crowd every week. There will be faithful fans there, but I think the atmosphere could be more like a Super Bowl than the Black Hole.

—Tom Flores,
September 2012, 2017

FOREWORD

Nearly every player who has worn the Silver and Black is proud to say that he's a Raider. There have been players who played for an organization for 10 years or so and then played for the Raiders for only one or two seasons, but the Raiders became their team for life.

That comes from how you're treated, starting at the top. Al Davis lets the players be who they are, as long as they play football on Sunday and as long as they win of course. We had great players when I was there. I can't say enough about them. They were terrific players. Sure, they were wild in their own way. We had a few guys who stayed out late at night, if not all night at times, but they went to practice and they worked hard. I had a great time.

It certainly wasn't much fun as an opponent of the Raiders. I say that from experience. There was an intimidation factor. The Raiders wore those larger shoulder pads and that made them look bigger. They wore black most of the time, and they looked meaner and scarier. You couldn't get around that intimidation factor.

One of the things I noticed when I got to Oakland—and I probably sensed it when I played against the Raiders—was that every time those guys stepped onto the field, they expected to win. It didn't matter who they were playing. It didn't matter how far behind they were with two minutes left. They felt they were going to pull it out. It was so incredible to be around that confidence. It was cool to finally get there.

I wouldn't trade my time as a Raider for anything else. I had a great time at New England when I first got there as a rookie, but eventually that wore out. I went to San Francisco, and I wanted that to work out more than anything in the world because I was back home for the first time, close to family and friends. Unfortunately, it seemed like the harder I worked there, the worse things got. That was a big disappointment for me.

Then I wound up in Oakland. Thank goodness I did, because it was a perfect fit. I was getting older and I couldn't take a rah-rah, drill sergeant type of coach, and the Raiders weren't at all like that. John Madden was the head coach when I first signed there in 1978. Before the next season, John retired and Tom Flores was promoted from receivers coach to head coach.

Tom was a quiet man who had a tough job, following in John's footsteps. However, Tom more than lived up to the task. He wasn't very vocal, but for me, he commanded respect, and, for the most part, he got it.

He was such a stoic man, but he had to work with a bunch of personalities day in and day out. I'm sure it wasn't easy to deal with all of these different characters, but he handled everybody the way they needed to be handled. I mean, who's going to tell John Matuszak what to do when he doesn't want to do it? Well, Tom Flores, that's who.

Some coaches go into a locker room at halftime and start yelling, but it doesn't mean anything. Some go in there and yell and it does mean something. Tom, on the other hand, was a man of few words. There were times when, after halftime, guys might turn to each other and one of them say sarcastically, "Nice halftime talk; way to get us fired up."

The thing that stood out with Tom is how he got us ready to play, especially mentally—knowing what to do and when to do it. He brought the Raiders a lot of success. One of the reasons why he was so successful was his preparation. He found ways to take advantage of the opponents' weaknesses. He knew how to get his teams ready to play.

Jim Plunkett and me at a golf outing. *Photo courtesy of Tom Flores.*

Coaching is a very difficult job and it was likely more so when Tom coached than it is today. Players make so much more money today and the makeup of teams is so much different. For instance, the Christian group of men in the NFL is much larger, or at least more known, than it was back then. Before, teams were a collection of different personalities, each doing his own thing. Tom knew how to get a lot out of the players.

In fact, one of the stories that Tom included in this book regards his involvement in a situation at the end of training camp in 1980, when I told him I wanted either to be traded or released. I didn't feel as if I was getting the opportunity to compete for the starting job. I had been on the bench behind Kenny Stabler for two years, and I felt that I was gaining my confidence and learning the offense, but I wasn't given the opportunity to start. The first year, I could understand, because I had been released by San Francisco. I joined the Raiders after the season started and Kenny was the man. In 1979, though, I should have been given a shot, I thought.

Then, before the 1980 season, the Raiders traded Kenny for Dan Pastorini, which was a No. 1 for a No. 1. Still, I was a No. 1 at one time and I had been with the Raiders longer than Dan, so I felt I should have been given the chance to compete for the starting job. It didn't look like that was going to happen. That was my tenth year in the league, so if I didn't have a chance to compete for a starting job somewhere, my career was pretty much over. If I wasn't going to have that opportunity in Oakland, I wanted it somewhere else.

During my career with the Raiders, Tom was a good mentor for me. He was the receivers' coach, but since he had been a quarterback in the NFL, he knew what I was going through. He had experienced a similar situation. He was a big help to me. He was someone to whom I could voice my grievances and he understood.

He was good enough to me to go tell Al how I felt about the situation. He came back and said, "Mr. Davis says no, we're not going to trade you, because we don't have an experienced quarterback backing up the starter."

Foreword

I wasn't thrilled with that decision at the time, obviously, but I stuck it out. Looking back, I'm very happy that I stayed.

Later in the book, you're also going to read about many of the players who played with and for Tom. One of the players is Jeff "Barnesy" Barnes, who was a linebacker from the late 1970s through most of the 1980s. Barnesy had a certain way of saying things sometimes, and we called them "Barnesisms."

You'll get a chance to read one of Tom's "Barnesisms"—which I believe I told him—and a few that I remember. Some Barnesisms seem exaggerated, but they're not . . . too much. Some Barnesisms can't even be described. It could be said that I make a living off Barnesy, because parts of my speeches feature Barnesisms. I love Barnesy to death, but he's easy to pick on.

You'll also read Tom's stories about some of the great Raiders, such as Fred Biletnikoff, Billy Cannon, Bo Jackson, Howie Long, and Jim Otto.

Tom offers his memories about the Raiders' early days in the American Football League, plus the Super Bowl years.

Tom is a great person to write *Tales from the Oakland Raiders Sideline* because he has lived these stories. He personally knows the people involved. He may not know every story from the history of the Raiders, or he may have a different perspective than someone else, but he's been an important part of the organization and what it is today. Plus, he coached at a time when the team had so many characters. He happened to be part of that collection of characters.

Only one person in the world has experienced the Raiders from the eyes of a player at the beginning of the organization, as an assistant coach, a head coach and a broadcaster: Tom Flores. I'm proud to say that I played for him and I'm honored to have him as a friend.

JIM PLUNKETT

ACKNOWLEDGMENTS

As with most books, there seems to be too many people to thank. However, if we didn't thank anyone, this would be a blank page. So to give you your money's worth by filling this page, the authors would like to thank the following personally for their hard work, dedication and support during this project:

To Erin Linden-Levy, Bob Snodgrass, and the rest of the gang at Sports Publishing for their patience, guidance, and desire to make this book the best book possible.

To the Oakland Raiders organization, particularly Al Davis for his support, Al LoCasale for securing many of the photos, and Craig Long, Mike Taylor and the media relations staff for their research assistance.

To Julie Akhlaghi, Rick and Amy Allen, Tim and Amy Brown and Tom Lawrence for transcribing, editing, equipment "rental" for the top of a mountain and overall support of this project. Your friendship is appreciated more than you know.

To Jim Plunkett for your willingness to write a great foreword and for sharing some "Barnesisms."

We each would like to thank our parents, brother, and extended families for their encouragement throughout our lives. Finally, Tom would like to thank his wife, Barbara, twin sons, Mark and Scott, and daughter, Kim, and grandkids Brian and Kevin, Jillian and Meghan, and Jacob, for being supportive throughout this project and his career. Matt would like to thank his wife, Libby, and children, Helen, Charlie and Aaron, for their support and understanding as we approached deadline. Thank you, all.

INTRODUCTION

The Raiders. Tom Flores. The words seem interchangeable. In many ways, they are. Whenever one is mentioned, the other is likely to follow. Since the beginning of the organization's history, Tom has been synonymous with the Raiders and championship football.

As one of the original Raiders players, Tom was instrumental in many of the organization's early wins and helped provide the building blocks for future quarterbacks. As an assistant coach under John Madden, Tom helped lead them to their first Super Bowl victory. As a head coach, Tom took two more teams to the Super Bowl and won. Today, Tom keeps his Raiders ties as the color analyst on the team's radio network.

Throughout the years, as with so many other Raiders players and coaches, Tom remains loyal to the "Silver and Black." That's how it works with families. That's how it works with the Raiders.

When I first heard the idea of *Tales from the Oakland Raiders Sideline*, it seemed like a great project. After all, I had worked with Tom during a Super Bowl book for CBS Sports, and he seemed like a nice enough guy. Working with him on this book, however, I came to realize how lucky Raiders fans and the entire Raiders organization are to have Tom as one of their own.

Indeed, he is a genuinely nice guy, but he is also a great football man who cares about his players and the organization for which he has worked most of his adult life. He meticulously picked stories that he felt you, the reader, would enjoy, while at the same time choosing ones that properly displayed the class of the Raiders' franchise.

If you are hoping to discover some dirt on the Raiders, put down this book and walk away. If you are hoping to read some great stories—oftentimes hilarious, sometimes poignant—about this proud organization, told by someone who lived the experiences, then keep reading.

There is no doubt that the Raiders have had more characters than any other franchise in the National Football League. Those characters, along with great coaches such as Tom and John Madden, helped turn the Raiders into one of the NFL's most successful organizations. On the pages that follow, you're going to learn more about the Raiders' remarkable history and the people who have made it wonderful, through the eyes of someone who is synonymous with the Silver and Black.

M.W.F.

TALES FROM THE
OAKLAND RAIDERS
SIDELINE

1

IN THE BEGINNING

The Oakland Raiders were one of the original American Football League (AFL) franchises when Lamar Hunt started that league in 1960. Other people who were instrumental in getting the league off the ground were Ralph Wilson with the Buffalo Bills, Bud Adams with the Houston Oilers (now the Tennessee Titans), Barron Hilton with the Los Angeles Chargers (now in San Diego), and several partners in Oakland, including Chet Soda and Wayne Valley. Actually, the Oakland franchise started out in Minneapolis. However, the city of Minneapolis withdrew from the AFL after it accepted an offer from the NFL to expand there. So the AFL selected Oakland to take Minneapolis's team.

NAME THAT TEAM

Oakland had a contest to name the team. Many people were sending in their requests and suggestions for names, with the winner getting a trip for two to Hawaii. The winning name was Señors. And for a month, the team was known as the Oakland Señors. What a terrible name! Fortunately, the organization realized that Señors wasn't a good name, and they decided to change it. Thank goodness for that—we were so bad in those early years that we would have been called the Oakland Señoritas at some point. Fortunately,

Original Raiders revisited. Wayne Hawkins (right) and I (left) share some laughs with one of the Raiders' original owners, Wayne Valley. *Photo courtesy of Tom Flores.*

the people in charge decided that Señors was not going to be a good name. I don't know how they did it, but I'm glad they came up with the Raiders. The new team was born. So we were the Oakland Raiders, playing in San Francisco at Kezar Stadium and then at Candlestick Park, living in Oakland and practicing in Oakland.

THE ORIGINAL SILVER AND BLACK

In the early days, the team was signing anybody it could possibly sign, especially trying to compete with NFL teams. The Raiders needed bodies.

2

If you could walk, you could be signed. If you played football in college or in the NFL, they definitely would sign you. They would sign former NFL players, Canadian players, and guys like Eddie Macon, from College of the Pacific, and Tony Teresa, who played at San Jose State before the San Francisco 49ers. Charlie Hardy, who also played at San Jose State and had a brief tryout in the NFL, was one of our ends. Bob Dougherty, a linebacker from Kentucky who played in the NFL, was an original Raider.

And then they signed guys like me. I had tried out in Canada but had surgery on my shoulder. Then I tried to make it with the Washington Redskins but failed. I actually was working on my master's degree when the Raiders contacted me about trying out. I figured, why not? I hadn't played in a while, so I was concerned about whether my shoulder would hold up, but it did.

Jim Otto, an undrafted player out of Miami, was an original Raider. Wayne Hawkins, out of the College of the Pacific, signed.

So, all in all, we had a lot of players and a lot of players who had decent talent. I am proud to look back and realize that I was a part of something great for the city of Oakland.

SO, THIS IS THE AMERICAN FOOTBALL LEAGUE

During our first season, we didn't have mini-camps, rookie camps, or anything like those that players have today. We simply were told to report to Santa Cruz, California, in early July for training camp. We reported and stayed in a hotel in downtown Santa Cruz, the Miramar, which was like an old retirement hotel. People in the lobby just stared into space, which reminded me of a retirement home. I found out later that it was a retirement home for some people. As one might imagine, there were not a lot of high-priced hotels in Santa Cruz in 1960. There were a lot of bungalows and vacation spots.

We got three meals, a bed, a television, and we could walk to practice. The food at the Miramar, however, was atrocious. After a while, we ended up eating pizza or something else, anything to avoid eating at the hotel.

We practiced at Santa Cruz High School, which was about a half-mile walk. Nobody seemed to complain about that. Actually, nobody complained about anything, because we were doing what we wanted to do. All of us realized that playing in the AFL was our last chance to play professional football—in some cases, our only chance.

Personally, I figured, what the heck. I was not married at the time. I had my education. I had my teaching credentials. I felt I might as well give it one more chance, and if I didn't make it, I would go on with the rest of my life.

SURVIVAL OF THE FITTEST

The first day of camp was picture day. There were 11 quarterbacks in camp, and the photographer was trying to get all of us in the same picture. It seemed impossible, but he did it. We had a barefooted kicker who got the most pictures. Ironically, he lasted about three days before being cut.

We had one day of practice, and then the next day, we went from 11 quarterbacks to four. Two of the seven were moved to other positions and the other five were released.

Eddie Erdelatz, our first coach, played and coached at St. Mary's College, which is close to Oakland. He made a name for himself at Navy, where he was successful before coming to Oakland. Eddie didn't feel a need for long practices. So our practices were very short, maybe a little more than an hour in the morning and a little more than an hour in the afternoon.

We never ran sprints during training camp, but we ran everywhere we went. We ran from one drill to another, and if a guy didn't do it at full speed,

Picture day, 1960—with (from left) me, Babe Parilli, and Paul Larsen.
Photo courtesy of Tom Flores.

he had to go back and do it again, and this time by himself, while everyone watched. It always was fun when a new player came in who didn't know the routine. Eddie loved to make an example of the new guy. We were in the best shape of any team, even though we didn't have the best talent.

Three of us survived the entire existence of the AFL: Jim Otto, who weighed 218 pounds as a rookie, but grew to 245, at center; Wayne Hawkins, who went from 230 pounds as a rookie to 260, at guard; and me at quarterback. We played 10 years in the AFL until the merger. Wayne and Jim were with the Raiders that entire time, and I would have loved to have been also, but unfortunately I was traded to Buffalo and then signed with Kansas City in 1969. Luckily, that was a Super Bowl year for the Chiefs, so I got to take part in Super Bowl IV. However, I would have preferred to stay in Oakland and be a part of their success, because I was a part of the early group. Things just didn't work out that way.

The last year of the AFL was 1969.

FIRST GAME

Our very first game was at Kezar Stadium in San Francisco. Many Raiders fans think that the first game was in Oakland at Frank Youell Field, but it wasn't. The very first game was in Kezar on July 31, 1960. It was a night game against the Houston Oilers, which we lost 37-22. And so it started for the Raiders.

ALAMEDA NAVAL BASE

In 1960, we didn't have a facility in Oakland to practice in or to play our games in. After we broke camp that season, our home became the Alameda Naval Base. The reason we went there was that Eddie Erdelatz had coached Navy and he had some connections, which allowed us to use the facility. It

In the Beginning

Eddie Erdelatz, our first coach, enjoyed more success at Navy than he did with the Raiders. *Photos courtesy of Tom Flores.*

actually was a good deal. Not that fans were trying to tear down the walls to see us yet, but obviously it was a secure facility. Once we drove through the gates, we didn't have to worry about security. We ate at their chow hall, their commissary, where the prices were reasonable and the food was quite good. Then we practiced on a field right there on the base and used their locker rooms.

The only setback was that our practice field was right next to one of their runways, where the big jet fighter planes would take off. Imagine being in the middle of practice, working on a play or going through a drill, and having to stop frequently and wait for the jets to take off. Once a jet took off, we could continue with our practice.

7

We were so close to the runway that we could feel the heat when the engines revved up and the planes took off. We couldn't hear ourselves think at all. In fact, that probably was the precursor to crowd-noise drills.

Years later, we tried to emulate noises so loud that players couldn't hear themselves think, so that would have been a great start for it. However, I would not recommend it to anybody. That noise at the Alameda Naval Base was so loud and the heat was so intense at times that it was very unnerving.

JOE FOSS

Joe Foss was the first commissioner of the American Football League, in 1960. After becoming commissioner, Joe made the rounds to every training camp. Of course, we're talking about only eight teams—Oakland, the Boston Patriots (now New England), the Buffalo Bills, the Dallas Texans (now Kansas City Chiefs), the Denver Broncos, the Houston Oilers (now the Tennessee Titans), the Los Angeles Chargers (now in San Diego), and the New York Titans (now the Jets).

Joe came around and gave more of a military-type pep talk. None of us knew his history, but those of us who were interested soon found out.

Joe, who was from South Dakota, was a fighter pilot in World War II. Not only was he a fighter pilot, he was one of the most decorated pilots during the war. Since I was growing up during World War II and we didn't have a TV in my house until I was a senior in high school, I didn't know about Joe and his heroics.

Joe was a remarkable guy. I really liked him. I liked his toughness. I liked his positive and gung-ho attitude about the AFL. In his talks, he compared being a part of our young league to going to war. Obviously, we were playing for fun and the passion of the game, because we weren't making a lot of money. He, on the other hand, was fighting a battle. Semper fi!

The most impressive thing about Joe was that long after he had left the AFL as the commissioner, whenever our paths crossed, he always made it a point to come over and say hello. He remembered those of us who were the pioneers, who started in the very first year of the Raiders. Joe always was proud to be the first commissioner of this league that became bigger than life.

When Joe passed away in 2002, the league lost a great ambassador. The country lost a great hero.

TOO BAD WE DIDN'T HAVE THE MONORAIL

The American Football League (AFL) was small in our early years. We typically were known as the "Mickey Mouse" league. Nearly every team in the AFL was a low-budget operation and traveling was done at the minimum expense. We took regular flights, not charters. To cut down on costs, when we traveled to the East Coast, we would take one flight out, stay for two or three games, and then fly back—possibly stopping someplace like Kansas City for another game.

When we were on the East Coast, we took buses and trains between Buffalo, New York, and Boston. When we played the Texans in 1961, we went back east and played the three teams, and then went from Boston to Dallas. We were gone for four games. I think we were gone a total of 20 days. This carried on through the existence of the AFL.

Travel was disorganized, but we always managed to get to the stadium on time.

I particularly remember one trip. We played a preseason game in San Francisco on Friday night, then flew to Buffalo for a game with the Bills on Tuesday, and then went to Boston for a game against the Patriots on Sunday.

Getting from San Francisco to Buffalo wasn't a problem. From there, it wasn't so easy. After the Buffalo game, we were driving toward Boston, and no one knew where to go. We just knew we were headed toward Amherst, which is where we were going to play the Patriots. (Of course, we didn't know where we were supposed to go because our travel agent was still in New York City, probably partying it up, having a good time.)

We were going through the town of Holyoke, Massachusetts, when we pulled up in front of an old hotel. Eddie Erdelatz went in to ask about rooms. Of course they had rooms. The look on the guy's face was as if he were thinking, "Heck, who in the world would want to stay in this place?" So we piled out of the bus, went in, unpacked, and piled back into the bus in search of a practice field.

We drove around until we found a Little League park for practice, and then found a public restroom to get ready in. Guys were on the lawn of the park, wearing their jock straps, being taped for practice.

So we got dressed and started practicing. A short while later, a crowd gathered to watch us, or at least that's what we thought. We had been practicing for about an hour when the local police came. We didn't know what was going on. But we had to get back on the bus and go back to the hotel. Come to find out, the Little League was about to get started. We just thought they were watching, but apparently they were getting ready to play. So Little Leaguers chased off our professional football team.

The food at this hotel in Holyoke was so bad that Eddie Erdelatz put us all on the bus and took us all to a restaurant for a nice steak dinner. I don't know if he paid for it out of his pocket or if he put it on the expense account, but it was like heaven. We ate so poorly at the hotel.

The day after being chased off the field by the Little Leaguers, we drove around and found another place to practice. Keep in mind, this is happening on Thursday, Friday, and Saturday before Sunday's game. We finally found out how to get to Amherst, so Saturday morning we jumped back into the bus and headed to Amherst. When we got there, the people that were in charge of the game said, "Where have you guys been? We've been waiting for you all week. We had dorms and everything set up for you at Amherst." Shoot, I don't know why they didn't send out the police to find us or something. We would have been easy to find. After all, we were whooping and hollering it up in Holyoke.

GOING HOME

Traveling back then always was an experience. When we started using charters, they were not the huge airliners. Smaller planes were used. We weren't traveling in DC-10s as the Raiders do today. Of course, we had fewer players at that time. The first year, 1960, we had 35 members to a squad. The next year, we dropped to 33. In the late 1960s, we were up to 37. So a big plane would have swallowed us up anyway.

Even though we used unknown charters, we still felt safe and the planes got us to our destination.

ALWAYS HAVE CAB FARE

During one trip, we were going from New York City to Boston. None of our four coaches was on the trip because they were scouting. At least, I assume they were scouting. So it was only about 35 players, our trainer George Anderson, and an equipment man on the train for Boston. (We maybe had a doctor if he was around, but that's another story for another time.) We knew we were going to be staying in Boston at the Kenmore Hotel, but we didn't know where to get off.

Finally, George suggested we just get off at a station. We all got off and found cabs. (We made sure to get a receipt so we could be reimbursed—remember, we weren't making much money.) We all ended up at the hotel where our rooms were waiting. Unbeknownst to us, the buses were waiting for us at the next train stop.

However, once again, our travel agent was in New York having a good time and our four coaches were out scouting.

Looking back, it's easy to see why we were exhausted when we came back from all our trips.

ATTENTION, PLEASE

As I mentioned, in the early days of the AFL, we flew commercial, just buying a certain number of seats on a flight. One trip when we were at the airport in Boston, an announcement was made over the loudspeaker: "Will the Oklahoma Raiders please report to gate four. Your plane is ready to take off." We assumed that was us.

BUFFALO TRUCK DRIVERS

In the old days of the AFL, we were not very well-known. People away from the West Coast didn't know who we were because not a lot of people knew where Oakland was. When we went to Buffalo, we stayed at Niagara Falls. In the evenings, since we were on the East Coast for three weeks, we usually were free, so we'd go out and have a few beers before curfew. By today's standards, our players weren't big, but back then they were. I usually went out with at least Jim Otto and Wayne Hawkins.

While we were out one night, some people came up to us and asked what we did for a living. They asked if we were truck drivers. We told them we played football for the Oakland Raiders. They asked us where Oakland was, and we told them. Then they asked if we were professionals. (We had to think about that one, because there was some doubt about the stability of the league.) That wasn't an unusual conversation. We reached a point where sometimes we'd play along and tell people we were truck drivers. People believed it and started up some conversation. We had fun because it was total BS. The stories would get better and better with the more beers we drank.

PROFESSIONALS?

As one might imagine, when a league's teams are cutting corners anywhere necessary, salaries aren't very big. When the people in Buffalo asked if we were professional football players, it took a few moments to figure that one out based on what we were making. I thought we were professionals. At least we were being paid to play. The minimum wage if a player made the team was $6,500. Personally, I got $50 for each preseason game, $37.50 after taxes, and then $9,000 if I made the team.

Sure, we were professionals, even though in those days when the season started, New York Titans owner Harry Weismer was bouncing checks all over the city. We got nervous and took our checks to the bank immediately to cash them. Sometimes we had to wait while money was transferred. It was not a lot of money at the time, the high-priced players were making $10,000 to 12,000 per year.

We had to roll with the punches back then. We were playing for fun. We were in it because we loved the game. We certainly weren't in it for the money, because we weren't making much. I made that $9,000. Of course, if I had gone into teaching, as I was planning to do if I didn't make the Raiders, I would have made $4,900.

MORE SEAGULLS THAN FANS

My days at San Francisco's Kezar Stadium were cold and damp, plus the Niners were playing there at the time. The field was chewed up pretty good; it was not much of a stadium. We never drew many people to the game. We averaged probably about 10,000. It seemed as if we had more seagulls at the game than fans while we were at Kezar.

We moved to Candlestick Park late in 1960 and played there in all of 1961. It was open at one end, and it was windy, especially at that time of year. When we moved there, the crowd got smaller because we were not as good a football team, the excitement had worn off, and we were an Oakland team playing in San Francisco. In fact, we averaged probably around 6,000 at Candlestick during 1961.

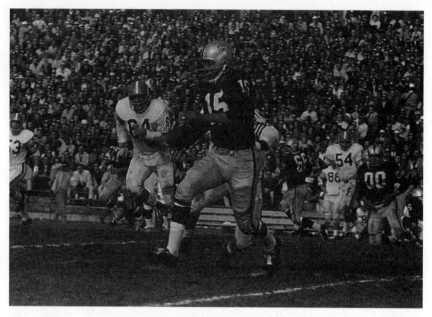

Speed kills—or at least it almost did me in during this game at Frank Youell Field in the early 1960s. *Photo courtesy of Tom Flores.*

DID YOU SAY OPTION, COACH?

We played Houston in 1960 in a hot day game. I think I lost 10 pounds during the game, and I only weighed 190 going into it. We played at old Jeppesen Stadium, where our dressing room was the boiler room. George Blanda was playing for Houston then.

We were practicing the day before, and Eddie Erdelatz wanted us to run the option. In professional football, that was unheard of unless your team had a running quarterback, and I was not a runner. Still, Eddie was an option guy. He was demonstrating on defense, and Babe Parilli, my backup, was at quarterback. Like me, Babe wasn't a running quarterback. But on this demonstration, Babe ran the ball and stepped on Eddie's foot, breaking his toe. That might have been the beginning of the end for Babe in Oakland.

We went on to beat Houston, 14-13, which was a big win at that time because we were off to a good start.

OH, RATS!

In New York, we had to leave lights on in the locker room at the Polo Grounds the night before, because if you didn't, rats and other creatures would be all over the equipment when we arrived the next day.

The Buffalo Bills continued to play at War Memorial Stadium, which had to be the worst place in the league. I didn't realize how bad it was, however, until I was traded there and played for them in 1967-68. The stadium, which was built right after World War II, was an armpit. It is known for two things: first it was the original home of the Buffalo Bills; second, it was the site of filming for *The Natural* with Robert Redford. Shortly after that, they finally blew it up.

OAKLAND RAIDERS . . . IN OAKLAND

After a successful 1960 season, we won only two games in 1961. I didn't think it could get much worse, but it did. The Raiders won only one game the next year. The good point was that we were finally in Oakland in 1962 at Frank Youell Field where the team played until 1966, when the Oakland-Alameda Coliseum was built. Finally, we were an Oakland team living, practicing, and playing in Oakland.

2

RIVALS AND FRIENDS

THE RAIDER HATERS

Of the Raiders' two main rivals—the Kansas City Chiefs and the Denver Broncos—I would say that the Chiefs rivalry is based on a mutual respect for each other. Sure, there have been some tough battles through the years, but the rivalry isn't largely based on dislike. The Broncos rivalry, however, is based on disgust.

There was a tremendous amount of talent on the field when the Raiders and the Dallas Texans (Kansas City Chiefs) played. Just look at the 1969 Super Bowl Chiefs and the playoff Raiders. Some of the game's best were on those two teams: Lenny Dawson, Jim Tyrer, Mo Moorman, Freddie Arbanas, Buck Buchanan, Willie Lanier, Bobby Bell, and on and on for the Chiefs. The Raiders had Gene Upshaw, Art Shell, Daryle Lamonica, Billy Cannon, and Fred Biletnikoff. Each team was practically an All-Star team. There was a lot of respect between the players of the two teams.

THE BEGINNING OF A RIVALRY

The rivalry started in the early 1960s when the Chiefs were the Dallas Texans. In 1961, playing at Candlestick Park, we had a huge fight. I was the quarterback, and I ran out of bounds in front of our bench. I was three or four yards out of bounds, and E. J. Holub, the Chiefs' linebacker, knocked me out even farther with a forearm. There was a huge fight in front of our bench. Guys were pushing, throwing punches, falling over benches—the works.

Since the AFL had only eight teams, we got to know players and teams pretty well because we might play them four times in one year. One year we played Kansas City in preseason in Seattle. That was Bobby Bell's rookie year. I realized how fast he was when I saw him on a play about 10 yards away, and then I took one step, turned and looked, and he was right there. I couldn't believe it!

I WAS ONE OF THEM

I joined the Chiefs after the third game in 1969, after being cut by Buffalo. Lenny Dawson had gone down with an injury, so I called Coach Hank Stram, and he said they'd take a look at me. I flew in that Tuesday, worked out, and signed a contract. I became a backup for the next two years.

It was a funny feeling walking into the locker room of the "enemy" for the first time, but all the guys were great. It was as if I had been there forever. The players made me feel at home. The Chiefs had a film reel of all their big fights. They showed me the reel of that infamous fight from Candlestick when I was quarterbacking the Raiders.

By the time I joined the Chiefs, E. J. Holub was the center. He was a wild and crazy guy. He told me, "Hell, Tom, you ran right into my elbow." I just shook my head. We talked about how that was one of the best fights between the Chiefs and the Raiders.

One of the Raiders-Chiefs games I remember was when I actually was with the Chiefs in 1970. We were playing at Municipal Stadium in Kansas City. In those years, it was always the Raiders and the Chiefs battling for the AFL West. On this particular day in Kansas City, we had a back-and-forth game.

During the course of the game, we (the Chiefs) had a play where, on a crucial fourth-down play and leading late in the game, Lenny Dawson faked the handoff, bootlegged, and picked up the first down. At the end of the play, Ben Davidson speared Lenny. It was blatant. The league didn't protect the quarterback as well as it does now. The hit was bad enough that today Ben would have been kicked out of the game and fined.

Anyway, Chiefs receiver Otis Taylor came from 30 yards away and jumped on Ben. The two had a pretty good scuffle, and the Chiefs were flagged for a penalty. So instead of picking up the first down, we were moved back 15 yards and ended up having to punt the ball. The Raiders moved the ball down the field, and George Blanda kicked a 49-yard field goal that tied the game, 17-17, which was the final score. George had a phenomenal year in 1970, but that one play did it for the Chiefs. A win in that game would have helped propel Kansas City to the playoffs.

That game was a pivotal game in the season because it was the first meeting between the two teams that year. The two teams were scheduled to meet again at the last game of the year. By all historical means, that game would have determined the AFL West. However, the Chiefs lost another game after that Raiders game, so the final game of the year was meaningless for them. The Chiefs were out of the playoffs.

HEY, I WASN'T THE ONLY ONE

I think I was the second player to play for both the Raiders and the Chiefs. Fred Williamson was the first player to go from the Raiders to the Chiefs. He was traded for David Grayson after the 1964 season. And then, in 1970, Billy Cannon went to Kansas City for a year.

Some of the other players have been with both teams, including Marcus Allen, Clemon Daniels, Rich Gannon, James Hasty, John Matuszak, Charles Mincy, Andre Rison, Bruce Pickens, and Harvey Williams.

BAD MOON RISON

Another Raiders-Chiefs game that I remember was a Monday night game in Oakland in 1997, when Marty Schottenheimer was coaching Kansas City and Andre Rison was playing for the Chiefs.

This time, the shoe was on the other foot, and the Raiders were ahead late in the game. There was so little time left in the game that they had to go for a touchdown in their next two plays. The Chiefs were driving but they faced third down and long.

Andre ran an out-and-up. The Raiders' cornerback and safety—who was supposed to be backing up the corner—both bit on the out move. Why? I don't know. The ball was thrown to Andre, who went in for a touchdown, and the Chiefs won the game, 28-27.

During the radio broadcast, when I saw the corner and safety bite, I just said, "Oh, no!" A remarkable thing about the play is that the corner, Eric Allen, and the safety, Eric Turner, were veteran guys—very good players. They should have thought, "If Rison was going for the out pass, then let him go and complete it. Then they have only one play left in the game." Instead, the Chiefs won.

LAMAR HUNT

I think Chiefs owner Lamar Hunt was one of the best, if not *the* best, owners in professional football. There is no question in my mind. He, along with seven other owners, started the AFL in 1959. At that time, I think Lamar was only 29 years old. Early on, when it was rumored that each of the league's teams was going to lose a million dollars, some reporters approached Lamar's father. They said, "Do you know that your son is going to lose a million dollars this year?"

Mr. Hunt thought for a while and then said, "Well, at this rate, he's only got 165 more years to go." That shows the kind of staying power that

Lamar had. Because of that and his dedication to football and the Kansas City Chiefs, who started out as the Dallas Texans, he was a real plus for professional football.

Lamar, along with one of his children, came up with the name Super Bowl for the NFL's championship game. In the early days, it was called the AFL-NFL Championship. (That's pretty original, isn't it?)

Lamar was married to a beautiful lady, Norma, who's a nice person. Lamar was highly competitive, and he had a great vision building the Truman Sports Complex in Kansas City, which includes the Chiefs stadium, Arrowhead, and the Royals stadium, Kauffman, a few hundred yards apart.

Even though the complex opened in 1972, you would never know it. Today, it's as nice as any complex in professional sports. Even though I played in Kansas City for only two years—playing with their Super Bowl team in 1969 and then in 1970—Lamar was more than hospitable to me. Any time I saw Lamar, he treated me as if I were a longtime member of their family. Much of that may have to do with the connection that AFL guys have with each other.

Loyalty was very important to Lamar. He was just a classy guy and a true gift to professional football.

HANK STRAM

Any time a book includes Lamar Hunt, it also needs to bring up Hank Stram. Hank was the original coach for the Dallas Texans. Not many people knew who Hank was when he started. Hank was very small in nature and stature but tremendously large in everything else that he did . . . ego included. We used to call Hank the "little mentor."

My experience with Hank was mostly from playing against him, except for the two years I spent with the Chiefs. Obviously, going to Super Bowl IV with the Chiefs, with Hank as the head coach, was an incredible experience. Even though I didn't play in the game, it was one of the biggest moments in my life.

Hank was so organized that everything was planned down to the exact minute. His leadership was extremely structured. He had certain rules. He even oversaw the way we dressed as a team. We all wore dark blazers with the Chiefs' arrowhead shield on the left breast, dark or light gray slacks, and a tie. That was our traveling gear. We had to wear that whenever we went on the road.

When the Chiefs first started, they had red blazers, but they changed to the dark blazers because they were at their hotel one time and some of the players were asked to carry bags to somebody's room. I guess some people thought they looked like porters in those red blazers. But there's no question, when you walk into a place and all you see is a sea of red blazers, it had to be a little distracting.

Under Hank's regime, everybody had to be clean-shaven—no mustaches, beards, or sideburns. The first day that I arrived, the team was getting ready to practice. I had long sideburns. I had signed a contract with the Chiefs after being released by Buffalo, where the rules weren't quite as stringent. Before I left Hank's office, he said, "Oh, Tom, we don't have long sideburns here."

I told him OK, already planning to shave them that night. Hank said, "There is shaving gear in the bathroom."

I realized he wanted me to do it right then. Of course, I had about two minutes to get out on the field. I asked him how short he wanted my sideburns. He said, "About where mine are." Well, he didn't even have any.

So I rushed into the bathroom, already dressed for practice, slapped some shaving cream on my face, and did the best I could to cut down about an inch on each sideburn and get them even. I knew they were not even. Plus I was bleeding because I did it so fast. When I finished, I grabbed my headgear and ran out the door.

When I got out the door, it was as if everybody was expecting me to come out looking like I did. I was bleeding, I had shaving cream on my face—it was obvious I had done it in less than a minute. All my new teammates were laughing and applauding. They knew exactly what I was doing. They knew that I needed short sideburns, but not one guy said anything about it—those rats! I was sitting right next to Lenny Dawson, and he didn't tell me. Mike Livingston didn't tell me. Buck Buchanan didn't say anything. No one told me. They just waited for it to happen because they knew it would.

One thing that incident showed me, though, was that I was accepted. That was good to know, considering I was a hated enemy for so many years with the Raiders. There always was respect and closeness in the entire AFL. I think that scene at practice was one way of welcoming me to the Kansas City Chiefs. I was just like them—no beard, no mustache, and no sideburns.

HANK'S INFLUENCE

To this day, I will say that Hank Stram has been vitally important in my career and my life. As a coach, you take a little bit from every guy, every coach, with whom you've ever played or been associated. That held true for me, particularly with Hank.

SUPER BOWL IV

My first exposure to the Super Bowl was in IV with Kansas City. Even though it was with the Chiefs—and was a Chiefs win—I want to tell a couple stories about that experience. In many ways, being around people like Hank Stram, Len Dawson, and others in that championship stayed with me in Super Bowls with the Raiders.

Today's pre-Super Bowl hype is generated by the media exposure. Whether there is one week or two between the conference championships and the Super Bowl, today there are various media days that players and coaches are "required" to attend. That hasn't always been the case.

During Super Bowl IV, in January 1970, the press days were quite different from today. Players stayed in their hotel rooms with their doors open, and if a reporter wanted to talk with a certain player, he would go to that player's room. The players just sat in their rooms, watching TV or whatever, waiting. That was it.

Reporters weren't seeking me out for an interview. They didn't really want to talk with backup quarterbacks—Mike Livingston and me. They mainly wanted to talk to Lenny because he was the starting quarterback and because there was a witch-hunt gambling investigation surrounding him.

We certainly didn't have the media circus that players have today.

WHAT A TRIP

During the championship game, unbeknownst to the players, NFL Films had miked Hank Stram. None of us knew until after NFL Films came out with the highlights and there was Hank in all of his glory.

Lenny Dawson was on a roll that day. We could tell early that there was no way the Minnesota Vikings were going to beat us. Since Lenny was playing so well, there was no chance that I was going to see action. Therefore, my main duty for the day was to stay on the headset with the coaches upstairs in the booth and follow Hank. He never got on the headset. He just said, "Stay with me. Stay with me. Stay with me."

So here I was, walking up and down the sideline with this headset and long cord. People were tripping over the cord. I was tripping on it, because Hank is just all over the place. He traditionally never stood still, but during the Super Bowl, he was strutting and prancing more than normal.

I was spending all my time trying to untangle the cord and dodge people on the sideline just to hang with Hank. I couldn't even pay attention to the game. Finally, I just waited in one spot, knowing that he would return. He did, with an emphatic, "How about that, boys? How about that, boys?" when a good play was called.

As he went into the Hall of Fame, class of 2003, he said it again . . . "How about that, boys?"

I KNOW THE FEELING

As most quarterbacks did in those days, Lenny Dawson called nearly all the plays. One of Hank Stram's more famous plays that day was one called "66 trap toss power trap," down on the goal line when Mike Garrett scored. It was huge. Hank went crazy. He was so fired up because a play that he called worked so well. I didn't know the feeling then, but I later found out how energizing that is.

In the AFC championship game against San Diego, before Super Bowl XV, I called a play similar to Hank's, using Mark van Eeghen. During our play, Mark might have been able to walk through the hole to the end zone. I didn't scream and yell like Hank did, but I certainly could understand why he was so excited.

Regardless of which team helps a player or coach get to the Super Bowl, that one day or night becomes a shining moment in his life. I know it was in mine, because there was no guarantee that I'd be back after Super Bowl IV.

MILE HIGH STADIUM

Did you know that Denver's Mile High Stadium was originally called Bears Stadium because the minor-league Denver Bears baseball team played there? It certainly was not much of a field. It also must have been used for rodeos sometimes, because there seemed to be cow manure on it occasionally. I'm not sure about that, though.

When we first started going there, before they improved Mile High, it had maybe 30,000 seats, and the visitors' locker room was actually about 75 percent dirt. They had one slab of concrete where the trainer set up his station and then all of the dressing accommodations were mostly on dirt. I think they did have a shower, though. It was a miserable place in 1960, but who cared? We would have dressed in a phone booth (which probably would have been better than the Mile High locker room).

In Denver, late in the season, those locker rooms were ice-cold. They did an incredible job of fixing that place up. And it lasted for many, many years, until their new stadium was opened recently. They've increased the seating over the years to 75,000 seats. They added luxury boxes and kept adding on and adding on, but it still was Mile High Stadium to me.

MILE HIGH FANS

There also were the many times that we'd be in one of the end zones and, before the Broncos had sense enough to put up the big fence, fans used to shower us with snowballs. That sounds innocent enough, except some of them were quite lethal because they had rocks in them.

The coaches' box was an open box that was even with the seats. So fans actually could stand up in their seats and look right in the box at your face. There were some interesting scenarios when some of our coaches would yell right at them. We could have punched some of those guys in the face. It was unfortunate when, once in a while, one of our soft drinks would accidentally slip over the edge and into the stands.

The coaches' box was way up on top, with no elevators to get there, so we ran up the ramp all the way, and by the time we got there at the end of the half, we were exhausted. We couldn't even breathe because of the thin air. Down in the press box, things weren't any better because if you didn't sit in the first row you couldn't see a long pass or a punt.

People can talk all they want about our crazy fans or how old our stadium is, but there was no place quite like Mile High Stadium.

THE IMMACULATE RECEPTION

People often ask me about my memories of the "Immaculate Reception," which happened during the 1972 AFC playoffs between the Raiders and the Pittsburgh Steelers. The Raiders were in the playoffs again, as they were for many years previously and would be for many years following. It also seemed as if every year during the playoffs, the Steelers and the Raiders went head-to-head.

In 1972, it was in their house. We had won the AFC West. The Steelers were starting to become the outstanding football team that they were in the 1970s. The game was on a cold, cold day. Two of the coaches and I were up in the booth and John Madden was on the sideline in his short-sleeved shirt—as usual. It seemed like he thrived in that kind of weather. Of course, that was his deal, too—short-sleeved shirt, tie, and his nametag on his belt buckle. As if nobody knew who he was and he was going to be kicked out because he didn't have a ticket for the game. I don't think so. (Dressing like that was one of his superstitions. Many of us had our own superstitions. We would sit in the same spot; we'd eat the same meal. Looking back, it was remarkable.)

Ken Stabler was our quarterback. Ken had started the season as the quarterback, and then Daryle Lamonica took over, and then Ken was back by the time we reached the playoffs.

In those days, every time we went to Pittsburgh, one of their groundskeepers, a heavyset, gruff guy, would yell and scream at John Madden about how they wouldn't let us on the field to practice. John would yell and scream back. Then they'd both start laughing, because that was their shtick. What the hell difference would it make, anyway; the field was frozen, for crying out loud.

But they really didn't want to let us on the field for practice this time because they were trying to keep it ready for the playoffs. So we made a big deal out of it, and John and a few other people in the organization got mad. The players usually went with the flow, so it was no big deal to them.

On this particular day, we had a low-scoring game. The seven points that the Raiders scored were from a long run by Ken in the second half. He ran about 40 yards for the touchdown. That touchdown put us up 7-6 with only a few minutes left in the game. The temperature was dropping, and I'd guess that the ground had long been frozen by this time.

Terry Bradshaw was trying to lead his Steelers' offense down the field. We forced the fourth down, and, as expected, they went for it. Terry dropped back to throw . . . this was it . . . the game's over . . . he scrambled to his right . . . we had him for a second . . . this had to be it. One of our defensive players, I'm not exactly sure who it was, tried to tackle him high, but Terry ducked underneath it. Terry scrambled back to his left and let the ball fly down the field. We were all watching, thinking it was over. Suddenly, the ball headed toward Frenchy Fuqua, who was going to be swarmed by Jack Tatum. The ball then bounced off somebody, and the game was over as far as we were concerned.

However, somehow Franco Harris was running down the field with the ball. Most of our guys were just standing around watching because they thought the ball was batted and that it was going to be incomplete. Jimmy Warren, one of our defensive backs, tried to tackle Franco at the last second, but by that time he was practically in the end zone, which is where he ended up.

The place went crazy. On the replay, you realize that Franco had picked up the ball that bounced off Frenchy or Jack, and caught it about two inches off the ground. Franco always seemed to be in the right place at the right time, which is why he's in the Hall of Fame. Anyway, there was bedlam on both sidelines and on the field. John was going crazy. Their sideline was going crazy. Terry was going crazy.

I'm not sure who the official was at the time, but there was a long pause before he made the decision that there was a touchdown. He actually went to the sideline and talked with somebody on the phone. To this day, I don't know why he did that. There was no instant replay in those days. Also, the rule in 1972 was that two offensive players could not touch the ball back to back, without it touching a defensive player first. So, evidently, the ruling on the field was that Jack had hit the ball and caused it to carom to Franco.

When the official finally came back and signaled touchdown, he explained the play to the crowd. I couldn't hear what he said because there was too much noise, as one would expect. Now, had there been instant replay, I don't know if the replay would have overturned the call, but it would have been nice to find out.

The Raiders were responsible for changing that rule. Now, two offensive players can touch the ball back to back, without it being a penalty, as long as it doesn't hit an illegal receiver first.

Nevertheless, had they reversed the call that day, I don't think I would have left the booth for quite awhile. I think I would have turned my jacket inside out to better match the all-black jackets of the Steelers coaches. It would have been a little dangerous walking back to the locker room had they reversed the call. But they didn't. The call stands, and to this day there are arguments about whether it was legal.

Months later, I heard through a reliable grapevine that the day after the game, Frenchy had a huge bruise on his left bicep. Jack was a hard hitter but his shoulder wasn't the force behind the left bicep bruise. I looked at every film that I could get my hands on, and it was hard to tell.

Bottom line is that we lost the game, 13-7, as Pittsburgh started making its mark in the playoffs. Ironically, that was the year that the Miami Dolphins went 17-0, which still stands as the NFL's only perfect season. They remained undefeated until the second game of the next season when the Raiders beat them in a game at Berkeley. Later that season, opening the playoffs, the Raiders avenged the 1972 loss to the Steelers, 33-14, before losing to . . . well, the Dolphins.

PAUL MAGUIRE

Talking about friends, I need to mention Paul Maguire, who is one of the funniest guys I have ever known in my life. He's also my best friend. Without a doubt, he's one of the most fun guys to be around, whether you're in the heat of battle on the football field, just sitting around having a beer—and he loves his Budweiser—or in some intense conversation. He is a neat person. He's honest and very intelligent. He's always trying to keep everything in perspective.

In my opinion, Paul is one of the best commentators, if not *the* best, in professional football right now. Even though he knows football is serious business, he understands that it's still a game. If something funny happens on the field, he points it out.

THE CITADEL

Paul Maguire is a great storyteller. Many people forget, however, that behind this funny and witty storyteller was a good football player. He was one of the most sought-after ends coming out of high school in Youngstown, Ohio. He could have gone just about anywhere he wanted, but he chose to go to The Citadel in Charleston, South Carolina. Interestingly, he went to The Citadel because Al Davis was an assistant coach, and he talked Paul into going there.

Before Paul went, he asked Al, "Do I have to wear a uniform?" And, of course, Al told him no. Paul asked, "Can I have a car?" Al said, "Yes, you can have a car."

So when Paul got to The Citadel, he found out that he had to wear a uniform. Then, when he went to Al about the car, Al gave him the name of a guy downtown to talk to about a car.

Paul said, "I thought . . . wait a minute, you mean I have to buy it?"

Al replied, "I said you could have a car. I didn't say we were going to buy it for you."

That was Paul's induction into The Citadel and Al Davis. He and Al were friends. Occasionally, Paul would call on Al for advice or other things.

When Al left The Citadel for the University of Southern California, he asked Paul to go with him. Paul refused to go, but two other players went with Al. Paul had made a promise to his father that we would remain and finish his college career where he started, which was The Citadel. He kept his promise.

Two of my great friends are Paul Maguire (center) and Jim Otto, here at the Raiders Boy Scout Tournament. *Photo courtesy of Tom Flores.*

GREAT FRIENDS

Paul Maguire and I have known each other since 1960. He was an original AFL guy, starting with the Los Angeles Chargers. He was traded to Buffalo in 1964. I just knew him casually in those days because we were always on the opposite sides of the field.

I really got to know him when I was traded to Buffalo in 1967. He and his wife, Beverly, became great friends to my wife, Barbara, and me.

3

RAIDER NATION

AL DAVIS

Everybody with whom I come in contact seems to want to know about Al Davis. I'm proud to say that not many people know Al the way those of us who have worked with him quite awhile know him. My only association with Al before his joining the Raiders in 1963 was by reputation. I didn't have any type of relationship with him until he came to the Raiders as the coach and general manager.

His reputation probably should have been a sign of things to come for the organization, because he was known as tough, knowledgeable, and enthusiastic, with a tremendous amount of enthusiasm about winning. And when he arrived, his philosophy on football was like a breath of fresh air to me. As a quarterback, if you didn't like his philosophy—throwing the ball and throwing the ball to everybody down the field—then you needed to find another position.

I missed the entire 1962 season because of tuberculosis. Some of Al's talent people advised him to go elsewhere for a quarterback. He told them no, that he was going to stick with Cotton Davidson and me. Since that time, Al and I have been through quite a bit. Here we are, three decades later, and we've been to four Super Bowls together—one when I was an assistant, two when I was the head coach, and one as a radio broadcaster (Al had a lot to do with my being hired there). I think we've gotten to know each other quite well during that time.

Therefore, I'm obviously not going to bash Al, but nor will I sugarcoat things. Al deserves better than either of those extremes. It seems that most articles about Al find a way to bash him. Either he doesn't give enough interviews or he doesn't do enough in public. Hey, many of the things he does just don't receive notoriety, which is fine with Al. That's his nature. He's secretive. He's a vicious competitor. Most people know both of those things. I want to point out the side that only a few of us have been able to see.

THEN THERE WAS AL

As soon as the dismal 1962 season—when we won only one game—was over, coach Red Conkright was fired. In January 1963, Al Davis was hired as the Raiders' head coach and general manager. Al was kind of an unknown to the public world. He had been an assistant coach with the San Diego Chargers since their start in Los Angeles in 1960, coaching the wide receivers.

Al was known for his great recruiting ability. He coached at the University of Southern California before the Chargers, and at The Citadel before USC. Wherever he coached, he left his mark as a recruiter. He was a dedicated and relentless coach in his desire to win football games.

Since I missed all of the 1962 season with tuberculosis, the first time I met him there was some skepticism as to whether I would be able to play again. In those days, we didn't have off-season camps, weight programs, mini-camps, or anything, so he didn't have a way to evaluate me. Players

We could tell we were in good hands when Al Davis took over as head coach in 1963. Al brought a great intensity and desire for winning to Oakland. Here he is on the sidelines (in tie) with Clem Daniels (36) and Jim Otto (00). *Photo courtesy of Tom Flores.*

got together with whomever they could find, trying to throw some balls and get into shape. Most of the guys did it on their own, so most guys would come back totally out of shape. We had six preseason games. Training camp was forever. I think we reported for camp shortly after the Fourth of July, and then we didn't break camp until the Friday before our first league game, which was September 7. Training camp was LONG!

During the off-season, Al had picked up Art Powell, Frank Youso, and Arch Matsos. He had picked up enough players that we had a decent-looking team. Cotton Davidson and I were the quarterbacks. Clem Daniels was our starting halfback. We finished Al's first season with a record of 10-4—quite a turnaround. We could tell the organization was in good hands.

NO TIME FOR *60 MINUTES*

Al Davis rarely gave an interview—very rarely. When he did, you'd better listen because it'll be a good one.

60 Minutes wanted to do an interview with him one time, but he wouldn't do it because *60 Minutes* can make the story go any way they want, and he knew that. He probably would have gone on had he been able to make sure that what he did and said came on, not what they wanted to come on. People in the spotlight have to be so protective these days because the media can slant stories any way they want. They can just take pieces of what is said, if they want. That's why coaches and players are so guarded, usually, before or after a game. Al's idea of handling the media, and our team dealing with its problems behind closed doors, has been wonderful for this organization.

RENEGADE OWNER

Al Davis had a passion for football. He never would do anything to hurt the game. Sure, he did some things attempting to get the edge on people.

Here I am with Al Davis (right) on the day I retired as the Raiders head coach, in 1988. *Photo courtesy of Tom Flores.*

Interestingly, some of the people who cried foul against Al probably have benefited from something he did. For instance, many owners tried to stop Al's move to Los Angeles and then back to Oakland. However, because of that move, no one threw a fit when Jim Irsay moved the Colts during the middle of the night from Baltimore to Indianapolis. He just packed up and everybody had to get out and move to Indianapolis in the middle of the night. He came in and told everybody to pack up because they were moving, and that was the first that many in the organization heard of the move. Art Modell didn't have much of a fight when he moved from Cleveland (Browns) to Baltimore (Ravens). Billy Bidwill moved the Cardinals from St. Louis to Arizona, and will probably move again if he doesn't get a stadium there. The Rams moved from the Los Angeles Memorial Coliseum to Anaheim to

St. Louis. Therefore, my point is that owners fought Al when he wanted to move, but they were thrilled to see that an owner could move.

Unfortunately, when we got down to L.A., a year or two after bringing them their first world championship football team, the new leaders of the Coliseum Commission said, basically, "We don't care what was promised to you to come down here, we're not going to do it." So, suddenly, here we go again. Of course, the other owners wanted to make a big deal about it again.

Simply put, Al was very loyal to those who were loyal to him. He would go to endless lengths to accommodate somebody—to help somebody—even if their departure from the organization was a little acrimonious.

I had one coach who became gravely ill. Al was the first one to send the coach to private doctors, to fly him there and anything else he could do. Unfortunately, we lost the coach, but Al was there behind the scenes making sure things happened to help save his life.

My wife took ill when I was working for the Seattle Seahawks, and Al was one of the first to call and make sure she had the proper medical attention. He wanted to make sure we didn't need anything. That's the way he was. When I left Seattle, once again, he was on the phone to see if we needed anything.

I won't say what he actually did for people, but he is extremely gracious. Stories have surfaced through the years about how people such as Elvis Presley secretly helped people in need. Al was very much the same way. However, Al was primarily concerned about people's well-being.

Even though Al was classified as a "renegade" owner or a "maverick," he had a tremendous following of loyal people. Former players and coaches from other places where Al coached are loyal to the Raiders because of Al.

Think of it this way. For each negative thing that so-called pundits say or write about Al, he did twice as many good things. (Many of these "experts" probably don't even know where to put the air in a football.) He did numerous great things for football and for people. Some people may argue with that, and so be it—that's their right.

CAROL DAVIS

There is one part of Al Davis's private life that I want to point out because it's worth noting in today's society. Al was very devoted to his wife, Carol, who was his friend, his confidante, and the light of his life. They were married for many years. They were very loyal to each other, and they both dedicated their lives to doing what's best for the Raiders.

MARK DAVIS

Mark Davis, Al's son, was a little guy when I first met him. Now he's a grown man. Regardless, back in the mid-1960s, when Mark was a young, redheaded, freckle-faced kid running around training camp, he wanted to play. He didn't know what was happening. All he knew was that his dad was out on the field with a bunch of guys, and they were all playing. Kids think that football is only playing.

My sons would ask me where I was going when I left for the stadium. I would tell them, "I'm going to go play football." So they asked their mother, "Why doesn't Daddy stay home and play with us?" So I had to change after that and tell them that I was going to work. Mark was the same way. He wanted to "play" with the guys on the field.

Mark was kind of a nosy and mischievous kid. During practice, he oftentimes would run on the field, grab the football and kick it, and then run right through the middle of a drill. Al would give him a stern look and say, "Will you get out of here?!" He would shake his head and mumble something, but then he'd smile because it was his son.

Mark always bugged all the players and the trainers in the locker room. One day—and I'll never say who did it—some mysterious people tied up

Mark and taped him to a chair in the locker room. They left him there for somebody else to find. He didn't cry; he simply looked around in bemusement, I guess, and went along with it until somebody came and cut him loose. I don't know how long it took the culprits to tape him, but it must have taken a lot longer to undo him with all the tape that was wrapped around. They had to have used several rolls of tape to wrap up little Mark Davis.

That was his first claim to fame during training camp. In fact, he probably was our first-ever training camp visitor to be taped to a chair in the locker room.

I think those years are when Mark developed his great love for the Oakland Raiders. To this day, he still lives and bleeds with the Raiders. With every loss he hurts, and, with every win, he celebrates. But I guess that's the way it is for most of us.

AL LoCASALE

One person who definitely deserves mention in a book about the Raiders is Al LoCasale. Al LoCasale spent 34 years with the Raiders as the executive assistant. He was in charge of the organization's administration. He was never involved in the coaching or personnel parts of the organization, but he was involved with everything else. He used to be somewhat of a liaison between Al Davis and the public.

Al LoCasale, who died in 2015, was a very bright man. He helped form the Chargers when they were first starting out in Los Angeles in the AFL. He worked for Sid Gilman, one of the great people in the history of professional football.

Al LoCasale was the first employee hired by the expansion Cincinnati Bengals. Paul Brown hired him as the team's director of player personnel. Paul was a remarkable guy and his legacy speaks for itself. In 1969, Al came to the Raiders.

Talk about working for some great people: Sid Gilman, Paul Brown, and Al Davis.

Al LoCasale (center) and me at the cermony on the steps of City Hall in Los Angeles, the day after winning Super Bowl XVIII. *Photo courtesy of Tom Flores.*

Al had a tremendous memory. He was in this game for so long that he saw some of the greatest moments and best players in the history of football. He was very loyal to professional football and to the Raiders.

If I ever had to run anything through anybody—a thought, a comment, an upcoming press conference—Al LoCasale was the guy I could talk to. When I became the team's head coach, he quizzed me on possible questions that the press might ask. His vast knowledge made him the guy who would help me. I could always go to him and run something by him.

He was the brightest guy to use as a sounding board for all the nuances away from the game that coaches have to be prepared for. I'll never forget that.

RON WOLF

I first heard of Ron Wolf in 1963, when Al Davis came to the Raiders. For a long time, many people in the organization probably thought Ron was a fictitious person. Many of us had heard the name Ron Wolf and we knew that he worked for the Raiders in some type of capacity, but we would have had trouble picking him out of a two-person lineup.

Who was Ron Wolf? Was he a figment of Al's imagination? Did Al make up this person so that he would have a name to which he could refer occasionally? Hey, maybe Ron was like that big rabbit in Jimmy Stewart's movie *Harvey*.

Well, we came to find out, Ron Wolf was a real person. There weren't many people in the front office or many titles in those days. (The Raiders never have been big on titles anyway.) Ron was always in the back room somewhere, in the darkness, looking at old films of teams and players. Or he was back there fixing the film when it broke, because in those days, the film couldn't handle the torture that scouts and coaches delivered with the help of the old Bell & Howell projectors—running them back and forth.

Finally, when Ron came out of the darkness, out of his mole hole back there and into the sunlight, we all said, "Ohhh, that's Ron Wolf." We realized Ron was playing an important role in the organization, because suddenly we would see this new player and then another new one. Ron was a big part of the Raiders organization and the development of the pool of players. He was almost like a one-man show establishing the scouting department and going around the country. He was doing a thankless job in those days. He wasn't getting much notoriety, but he probably didn't get much of the blame either if things didn't work out.

TAMPA BAY

Ron Wolf became better known to the football world during the 1970s, because when the Tampa Bay Buccaneers were formed, he became their first director of player personnel. He was responsible for building up the talent of that young expansion team. Unfortunately for Ron, he left Oakland one year too soon, because in 1976 the Raiders won their first Super Bowl, XI. The Raiders went to Super Bowl II in 1967, but they lost that one to Green Bay.

The first coach of the Buccaneers was John McKay. I point that out because a couple of years later, Ron and McKay had a clash, and one of them had to go. John had the upper hand, so Ron left.

Ron came back to the Raiders during John Madden's last year to help in the scouting department. Ron helped John with some of the personnel moves and doing some of John's extra work, taking some of the pressure off John. By that time, John, who was a high-stress guy, was showing some fatigue after coaching for 10 years.

A RING FOR RON

I remember in January 1984, when we were the Los Angeles Raiders, playing in the AFC Championship Game against the Seattle Seahawks. We had a comfortable lead—or at least comfortable enough that we were going to win—with about a minute left, and I was on the sidelines. I was not celebrating yet, but I was feeling good inside. I turned around and there was Ron Wolf with the biggest smile on his face, because now he had a chance to go to the Super Bowl. He was just beaming. He gave me a little nudge. I think if people hadn't been looking, he would have hugged me and we probably both would have cried a little bit.

It was great to win that game and then go on and beat Washington in Super Bowl XVIII, especially considering Ron was getting a Super Bowl ring. There is never any guarantee that you will reach that level again, which makes each one sweeter.

GREEN BAY

Ron Wolf had some health problems while we were in L.A., and he walked away from football for a short time. When he resurfaced, he joined the New York Jets as an assistant in the scouting department. Later in the 1980s, he got a chance to go to Green Bay. I was a little surprised that he took that job because he wanted to get away from some of the stress of being

A few of the people who have made this organization, at a game in Green Bay: (from left) George Blanda, Ron Wolf, me, Jim Plunkett, Al Davis, and Ted Hendricks. *Photo courtesy of Tom Flores.*

the head of a department, which is why he went to the Jets. Nevertheless, he took the challenge of Green Bay.

Quietly—the way Ron works so well—he started assembling a championship team in Green Bay. The biggest acquisition he made was getting Brett Favre from Atlanta. Brett had been injured in an automobile accident, and his health was a question mark, plus he had some other baggage that made him a little wild and crazy. The Falcons already had Jeff George at quarterback, and I know that coach Jerry Glanville told their director of player personnel that he didn't want Brett, for whatever reason.

We all make mistakes as head coaches. Getting rid of Brett was one of Jerry's biggest mistakes as a head coach. But a coach has to make a decision and live with it. Ron worked out a deal with the Falcons to get Brett in Green Bay. The rest is history.

Bringing Reggie White out of retirement was another huge move for Ron. He did a marvelous job of drafting and signing personnel. When Ron left, Green Bay went back to the way it was during the 1980s.

Now Ron is retired and probably bored to tears, but living very nicely. I won't say where he is living, but he and his wife, Edie, and their sons are probably enjoying themselves. I'm not sure what Ron's going to do in the future. I'm not sure how long he'll be able to stand retirement. He's not a golfer or a fisherman; he's a football man. His wife is a psychiatrist, so maybe that's what keeps him sane.

JOHN MADDEN

I went to work for John Madden in 1972 as the wide receivers and tight ends coach. Eventually, I coached the quarterbacks also, so I was primarily involved in the passing game. I got to know John from 1972-78. He had a remarkable career in Oakland.

John had an interesting personality. At times, he was very volatile, and then five minutes later, he would be the opposite, laughing and carrying on.

He was a tremendous competitor and very emotional. He was one of the best game-day coaches because he controlled the clock well, utilized the game plan, and handled the players well. The players liked him.

Obviously, John's biggest thrill as a coach for the Raiders was his Super Bowl XI victory against the Minnesota Vikings. We had had a great year even though we had gone from a four-man line to a three-man line because all of our defensive linemen were hurt and we had picked up John Matuszak that year. We played our best players, and we had enough good players—really good players—to win.

We lost one game that year. New England killed us, 48-17, in the fourth game of the season. During our coaches meeting the next day, John acknowledged that New England had beaten us easily, but maybe they showed us what we still had to do on a three-man line. We were too stationary, like sitting ducks.

They knew how to attack a three-man line because they used a three-man line team defense. So they showed us a few things that we had to work on to make sure that wouldn't happen again. Ironically, we played the Patriots again that season, in the first round of the playoffs, and beat them at the end of the game, 24-21. We then easily beat Pittsburgh in the AFC Championship Game, 24-7, before beating the Vikings in the Super Bowl.

I think John proved that season what a good tactician he was and how well he could handle the team.

PEOPLE PERSON

John Madden was a people's guy, and he still is to this day. He drives around in his big bus and enjoys visiting little towns. He likes to meet and talk with people.

John was very loyal to the Raiders. He started as a linebacker coach with the Raiders from 1967-68. He then became the head coach in 1969, and he stayed until 1978. John's loyalty was so strong to the Raiders that I don't know if he would have coached anywhere else. I don't think that his heart would have been with any other team.

He did not like to fly, so he doesn't any more. He doesn't have to; he has that big bus that he travels around in nowadays.

He's now doing what he was meant to do, which is entertaining people with his commentaries, doing commercials, and just overall enjoying life. It's funny, you might see him do a *Monday Night Football* game and then see him 500 miles away the next day, having coffee in a little diner. So that's John Madden; that's his life and he's enjoying it—and why not!

THE PRIDE OF THE SILVER AND BLACK

The players who have been with the Raiders for any length of time are very loyal. So if we're in a place like Kansas City and there are former players there, they'll come and visit. That's kind of a tradition because we're such a close-knit group of guys.

The group is not an open organization, because Al Davis prefers to have it closed-door. We don't air out any of our stuff in public. Disagreements or problems are handled behind closed doors. Historically, the Raiders have never responded to conjecture or innuendos about the team or Al.

RAIDERS FANS

Raiders fans are like no other fans in the NFL—actually, they're unlike fans in any other pro sport. Understand that everybody thinks their team has the best fans in the world, and they should. After all, there are the Cleveland fans with the "Dawg Pound." Denver fans have their "Orange Crush" and end zone noise. Kansas City fans have their "Sea of Red" and unbelievable noise. When the Seattle Seahawks played in the Kingdome, their fans were

My wife, Barbara, and me, lifelong friend Parris Farzar, and John and Virginia Madden, celebrate John's birthday in 1979. *Photo courtesy of Tom Flores.*

the "12th Man," and believe me, they were the 12th man, they were so loud. There were the white hankies in Miami, and the "Steel Curtain" in Pittsburgh.

Raiders fans, though, have always been unique. OK, I am not positive about "always," but I do know that they have been for most of the team's existence. At Frank Youell Field, where we played from 1962-65, you could turn around and you were no more than 12 feet from the stands. The fans were right behind the bench. The players could turn around and talk to

Raiders fans showed their patriotism following the 9/11 attacks in 2001. *Photo courtesy of the Oakland Raiders.*

them. We could almost touch them, they were so close to us. Only about 20,000 people could jam into Frank Youell Field, but their excitement and enthusiasm was felt because they were so close. During those early years it was almost as if they were in the game with us, especially in 1963 when we started winning.

The fans were also close to the visitor's bench. So once they started getting more vocal, teams did not want to come play us because of the yelling and the screaming behind the bench. I was on that side of the field a couple of times when I was with Buffalo and Kansas City. It was a hostile environment. However, it was not a dangerous environment by any means.

The perception is that the Raider fans are all criminals. They're not. Some of them may look like it, but so do some of those Denver and Kansas City fans. In our case, any time you dress in black you're going to look like a bad guy.

That rowdiness carried over into the Oakland Coliseum when we moved in 1966. Since the Raiders were winning during the late 1960s and throughout the 1970s and 1980s, that closeness was also carried over. During that span, we had a few guys who were starting to dress in "bizarre" outfits. But, again, that's in every stadium. Hey, our fans dressing the way that they do is no worse than the fans who shed their shirts and paint their bodies in below-freezing temperatures, or male fans who show up at games wearing dresses and pig snouts.

FAN FOLLOWING

Raider fans are forever. You either love the Raiders or you hate the Raiders; there's no in between. Early in the 2002 season, when we played at the San Diego Chargers, there were hundreds of Raiders fans in the airport who were in town just for the game. When we go to New York, Buffalo, New England, wherever, our hotel lobby is always filled with Raiders fans. That's just the way it is.

HALLOWEEN

Raiders fans have a love-hate relationship with the team. When the Raiders are winning, you love them. When they are losing, you hate them, but they are your team, so you don't criticize them.

Television added to the aura of the wild and crazy Halloween atmosphere at every home game, because the networks carried most of our games during the 1970s and 1980s all over the country. So the nation would see guys with skulls and crossbones and things sticking out of their bodies. Sure, the fans probably knew that they were going to be on television, so they would dress up. Then they would look into the television camera and snarl and yell. The personality just kept growing.

RAIDER NATION

I believe television is part of the reason why the Raiders are popular across the country. When we became a good football team, we were the second part of the national television doubleheader. All of our home games were at 1:00 Oakland time, or 4:00 back east. So fans on the East Coast or in the Midwest would watch us after they watched the early game. We were on TV a lot on the East Coast, and we became very popular because of that. Back then there weren't a lot of teams and no home satellite services.

Then, when we got guys like George Blanda, who went to Kentucky, and Kenny Stabler, who went to Alabama, we became popular in the South.

We became popular in the Northwest because before the Seahawks were in Seattle we played a lot of preseason games throughout the area. When it came to preseason games back then, we were like a barnstorming group trying to get fans and it worked.

It doesn't hurt that the Raiders have been involved in a lot of great games, or at least memorable games. The "Heidi" game was the Raiders. The "Immaculate Reception" was the Raiders. There was a stretch where we

Raiders fans like to have fun. *Photo courtesy of the Oakland Raiders.*

played the Pittsburgh Steelers so often in the playoffs and during the regular season that it almost seemed like we were in the same division. I think that's why Raiders fans are all over the country.

LOS ANGELES FANS

When we moved to Los Angeles, the fans were different. L.A. fans were a little more laid back. I don't think they really were ready to handle our normal types of fans. Many of the fans from Oakland went down to L.A. for the games. Those loyal, loud, and growly fans migrated south. Among the fans that people saw on television every once in a while were some prominent people or people with advanced degrees, such as doctors or lawyers.

Cleveland's Dawg Pound probably has some highly qualified business-men. They are not a bunch of derelicts. The same holds true with the Raiders.

The Raiders fans now have the "Black Hole," where they are famous for yelling and screaming. The people in those areas of the stands know each other. When people know each other, they are less likely to be outrageous toward one another or start fights and all that stuff. Fights at Raiders games usually are from one-timers who spent too much time at the tailgate parties.

Our first big game in L.A. was a 1982 playoff game. There were 93,000 people at the Coliseum. I don't know that the stadium personnel were ready for our kind of fan. Sure, they had hosted 93,000 before, but that usually was for a USC game with alumni and students, not Raiders fans. That was quite an experience.

In 1983, when we played in the first playoff game against the Pittsburgh Steelers en route to the Super Bowl, the stadium was just wild and crazy. There were some fights by guys who partied before the game. It boggles my mind why a guy would pay the kind of money that you have to pay to get a seat for any pro football game and then get drunk and not be able to enjoy the game. It is sad that people were so lit up that they didn't even enjoy the game. Of course, there was some celebrating after the game, too. They certainly did not have enough security to handle the next game, which was the AFC Championship Game against the Seahawks.

The L.A. people were ready with their police dogs, horses, SWAT teams, commandos, Navy SEALs, Rangers—just kidding. They seemed to have everything, though. There were some arrests, as usual, but overall it was a much better and more controlled crowd as we went on to win the first Super Bowl in the history of the Los Angeles area.

WHEN FANS ATTACK

Raiders fans sometimes get too much abuse by people from other towns. Every town has its semi-out-of-control fans—the handful that ruin it for the others. One of the worst tongue-lashings I have ever received was in Denver.

There was a fence between the fans and our bench, but I turned around and there was a guy yelling and screaming. I looked at him, which he evidently took to mean I was listening to him, and he proceeded to go off on me. I had never been berated like that. Ever. He just went on and on, including some personal things. I am not the type of person to react to a guy like that, but if I were, I would have gone after him. He was just so out of line.

Also in Denver, I was standing on the sideline during a game when all of a sudden, something whizzed by my ear. On the ground in front of me was a "D" battery. We're not talking a little, tiny "AAA" battery, but a "D" battery, which is a heavy-duty battery (especially when it's hurled from the stands). If that had hit me, it would have done some damage to the back of my head. Or, if I had turned to the side and had my face and eyes exposed—boy, that was dangerous.

Years ago at Kezar Stadium in San Francisco, one of their fans threw a beer can that hit John Brody in the helmet as he was going off the field through the tunnel. I guess there are stupid fans everywhere. Unfortunately, that small percentage of fans gets too much notoriety for being wild and crazy.

LOYAL TO THE END

Raiders fans might get mad at the front-office people for moving the team or at the players for not doing well, but Raiders fans are forever. The love-hate relationship will continue. However, as goofy as they might appear, they are tremendously loyal.

THE OAKLAND-LOS ANGELES RAIDERS

Moving from Oakland to Los Angeles in 1982 was not an easy task. When I took over as head coach, the rumors that we were going to L.A. had started. Then, all of a sudden, we were going, and then we weren't going. It was a roller-coaster time. After we won Super Bowl XV, during my second

The Skull Patrol was out in full force during the 2002 AFC Championship Game against the Tennessee Titans. *Photo courtesy of Tom Flores.*

year, my wife and I went to Hawaii for a little R&R. By the time we got back, everything had hit the fan.

I thought the people who operated the Oakland Coliseum were going to make the necessary changes to keep the Raiders. Instead, they told Al Davis that they weren't going to make any changes and that Al couldn't move the team because NFL commissioner Pete Rozelle wouldn't allow it. I think that was when Al went down and finally started listening to the people in Los Angeles. Negotiations began and were ongoing.

In 1981, we were the lame-duck team because we were destined to move to L.A. in 1982. We did not have a very good year on the field. Some of our players were on the downslides of their careers, so it was time to rebuild and add new life to our team. We finally did that in 1982 when we drafted Marcus Allen and Vann McElroy. Howie Long was in his second year, and we got Lyle Alzado. We were getting enough guys that we were starting to rebuild.

In 1982, we had planned on going to L.A. as soon as training camp broke. We had a facility down there and we had all the things in place, but the players' strike was looming.

The strike lasted eight weeks. There was some warning that it was going to be a long, bitter strike. The players were locked out. We, the coaches, worked out, did crossword puzzles, and went home at a decent, reasonable hour because there were no games. Every week, the games would remain scheduled and then be called off right before the weekend.

So every week we would put up the same game plan, look at a few tapes, and then go home knowing that there was no game. Finally, when the eight weeks were almost over, we got some information and a feeling that it was going to be settled. We made some preparations and then the decision was made that we would not completely move to L.A., but instead we would practice in Oakland and play in L.A.

So we practiced in Oakland and then every weekend we flew down to L.A. on Saturday for home games, played the game on Sunday, and then flew back on Sunday nights. That was tiring and tedious, yet we were 8-1 that year and made the playoffs. We were on the verge of having an outstanding football team, but then the season was over.

Still, we were living in Oakland and we were flying down to L.A. for different events, the draft, whatever we had. Then, we had training camp in Santa Rosa.

When we broke camp that year, we put all the cars on flatbeds for those who wanted their cars taken to Los Angeles, and then we all got on a bus, went to the airport, and flew to L.A. Some of my coaches and I lived in a hotel for 14 months.

That year, 1983, was a great time for us because we were winning, but it was not a glamorous time for us. I remember winning a game, going to the after-game party, and then taking my wife and daughter back to the airport. My daughter was crying because they had to fly back to the Bay Area since she was still in school. I went back to my hotel room at the LAX Hyatt and thought about this time of my life. Here we were, a championship team on the verge of going to the playoffs and, ultimately, the Super Bowl—which I didn't know at the time—and here I am in a hotel without my family.

To win Super Bowl XV in Oakland and then XVIII in Los Angeles in that short span, I think, is just a remarkable feat for the organization, the coaching staff, and the players. I don't know if anything like that had ever been done.

THEY CALLED HER "THE STREAK"

We've had some great players in the organization, obviously. Many of them have been tremendous characters and great pranksters. There was one practice during training camp when I was the head coach where the guys were lined up and getting ready to warm up. There was a strange feeling that something was about to happen. About that time the gate opened, and a nude lady ran down one sideline and then down the middle of the field. All of a sudden, she started running out of gas. She barely reached the gate and staggered out. I turned to one of the assistant coaches and said, "I think we've been in camp long enough. It's time to go home." I don't know how many guys were in on it, but obviously somebody got her to do it. It wasn't uncommon for guys to pull different pranks like that to liven up practice.

4

THE PLAYERS

MARCUS ALLEN

Marcus Allen was probably the most complete back I've ever seen. He could do it all. That made him even more fun to coach. When you have players who could do the things that he could, you can be more creative. Marcus did more than just run; he was a tenacious blocker. He was fearless. He could catch the ball in traffic. He had a great ability to do everything, and he did everything well. The only thing he lacked was blazing speed, but he certainly was not slow. He was involved in many big plays for us, whether he was running with the ball, catching, or throwing.

Many people may not remember that he was a fullback at USC, blocking as a sophomore for Charles White when Charles was a senior. Marcus moved to tailback during his junior and senior years.

Marcus was a quarterback in high school, and in college and the NFL he could throw the ball as well as most quarterbacks. Even going back to the 1950s, Marcus would have been one of the game's greatest single-wing tailbacks.

Rookie

We drafted Marcus, a Heisman Trophy winner, in 1982 in the first round. At that time, we were the Los Angeles Raiders. It was quite awhile, however, before Marcus made his home debut for the Raiders. In fact, he didn't play his first game in front of the home crowd until November. We all knew early in the season that the NFL players were going to go on strike and that it probably would be lengthy, so we were not going to go to L.A. until after everything was settled.

Our first two games that season were on the road against San Francisco and Atlanta. We started by beating the 49ers, 23-17. Marcus had a great rookie premiere that day. The next week in Atlanta Marcus had another good game, and we won big, 38-14. Then the strike hit for eight weeks.

Eight weeks of doing nothing except mock game plans. When we came back, Marcus didn't miss a beat. Everybody else was a little out of shape. Not Marcus. He continued to train with former UCLA track coach Jim Bush. After I found out about it, I hired Jim to work with our entire team. Once our players bought into it, most of them loved it. In the fourth quarter when Marcus was still running hard, most everybody else had slowed down a little. The great players are like that. Eric Dickerson was like that, but he had tremendous speed as well.

Instincts

Sometimes Marcus would react to shadows in practice. He'd make a move only because he caught a glimpse of a shadow. He was so instinctive. He also had great patience, which I think comes from his great vision. The great runners I've known, going back to college with Dick Bass, have that great vision.

If you asked Marcus why he made a certain move, he'd say he didn't know why, he just did it. That vision allowed him to be patient and set up his blockers. He was a great cutback runner. He was powerful and a tough son of a gun. He wouldn't back down from anybody, which also made him a great blocker.

Marcus Allen wasn't the fastest Raider; but he loved to run. *Photo courtesy of the Oakland Raiders.*

Versatility

John Robinson, who was my roommate for one year as an assistant with the Raiders, had coached Marcus at USC. The one thing John told me was, "Throw him the ball." We always loved to throw the ball to our backs out of the backfield. That was just a Raiders tradition. Sure enough, Marcus could catch the ball as well as anybody. He could also throw the run-pass. Our run-pass percentage of completions was incredible.

We had one play that we put in for Marcus, where he would run to his left and the quarterback would flip the ball to him as if we were running the sweep on a short-yardage situation. He would stop and Todd Christensen would roll around, pretend that he missed a block and then slip out and go deep. Marcus would stop and throw the ball back across the field. The ball was usually perfectly thrown. We practiced that once or twice a week. Sometimes Marcus' hands were so beat up and his shoulders ached late in the season, so we could not practice it, but it was still in the game plan and it was still a high-percentage completion play for us.

Run, Marcus, Run

Marcus played and practiced like a Mercedes. He always set the tone in practice. Sometimes it was annoying. Every time he ran with the ball in practice, he ran 40 yards. All the tailbacks at USC did that. So he was running 40-yard sprints every time he touched the ball, and then we had to wait on him to come back to the line of scrimmage, out of breath. Eventually I orchestrated it a little bit so that we wouldn't run him too many times in a row. Usually when we ran plays, we ran all of our running plays, then all of our play-action plays, and then our passing plays. Luckily, Marcus was in immaculate condition.

Never Let Them See You Cry

Marcus not only was an outstanding football player, but he also was a leader; he was a tough leader. We had a receiver who was hit right in front of the opponent's bench and he was lying there, moaning. Marcus went over and yelled at him to get up. The gist was, "Don't you dare lie in front of their bench and squirm. Don't let them know you're hurt." That was Marcus' motto. Even when he was hurting, it was hard to keep him off the field. Every time he came off the field after being banged up, I'd turn around and there he was hobbling back on to the field.

Once a Raider, Always a Raider

It's too bad that Marcus left the Raiders with ill feelings. I think that whole thing was blown out of proportion. A few things happened along the way that bruised egos. However, nobody's going to remember Marcus Allen as a Kansas City Chief. He's going to be remembered as a Raider because that's where he had his heyday. He had a good career in Kansas City, but he had a marvelous career with the Raiders. Marcus always will be remembered as a Raider.

LYLE ALZADO

On the other side of the line from Howie Long in the 1980s was Lyle Alzado. We picked up Lyle in 1982 from Cleveland. Lyle started in Denver, so we knew him pretty well. Al Davis always loved Lyle when he played for the Broncos.

The first time I saw Lyle was when I was scouting in 1972 at Yankton College during the off-season. It was about 20 degrees below zero outside and he was in the little gym working out. I had no idea who this guy was. I soon learned, because he was quite a player.

When Lyle came to camp at Santa Rosa, we put him at defensive end. Dave Browning was our first-team guy, so Lyle became second string. We really did not know if Lyle had anything left, because when we watched him on tapes from Cleveland, it looked like he was just going through the motions—rounding third base and heading for home in his career. At least, he had that kind of look in his eye. We hoped that we could jump-start him a little bit and get some more out of him.

I was sitting in my office one afternoon between practices at training camp in 1982 when Lyle came in with tears in his eyes and said, "Coach, I think I want to retire. I just don't think I'll be able to help you." We talked for a while, and I said, "You know, Lyle, give it a chance. Don't think that you can't help us. You let Al Davis and the coaches and me make the decision. If we don't think you can help us, we'll let you know. I know that training camp becomes boring, especially for a veteran who's been there so many times. Just do what you're doing, work hard, and get through training camp. Once we get playing, things will change."

Lyle was a fierce competitor, and he would go crazy sometimes. By the time things got going that season, we had no doubts that Lyle could regain his former status as a player. He became our number-one starter. After the strike that season, we were 8-1, and then we won our first playoff game. Unfortunately, we lost our second one against the New York Jets. But Lyle was back and playing well and enjoying life in Los Angeles. It was as if he were meant to be in Los Angeles.

As most everybody knows, we lost Lyle in 1992 to a brain tumor. His memory will live on. His legacy will live on. Lyle just couldn't get away from the steroids because everything about him was massive and he wanted to keep the bulk. Even after he retired from football, he kept using the steroids.

He left his legacy on the football field, and, perhaps, in a death linked to steroid use, he left his legacy off the field.

JEFF BARNES

Every once in a while, a guy like Jeff Barnes comes along. Jeff was an incredible athlete. He was about 6-foot-2, 225 pounds, and he could run like a deer. He could run, he had strength, he could jump—he did everything. He was such a great athlete. Jeff was about as good as they get on special teams and at rushing the passer from a linebacker location. He was great at the nickel package, which is a man-to-man defense. Jeff would lock on to a guy, and I don't care what happened around him, that was Jeff's guy. If the guy ran to the locker room, Jeff would chase him. If the guy went to the bathroom, Jeff probably would wait outside the stall for him. Get the picture?

Jeff was a fun guy. He had a great sense of humor, which is good because he had little sayings that we called "Barnesisms." For example, one time we were getting ready to go on a trip and one of the supply trucks accidentally ran into the wing of the plane. Of course, that delayed the flight. While we were sitting there, Jeff said, "Boy, it's a good thing that didn't happen while we were in the air; we'd have really been in trouble." Well, I've never seen a flying truck before. Perhaps Jeff had. Anyway, Jeff certainly could say things sometimes that made us give him a second look and left us wondering: "What did he say?"

MORE BARNESISMS
from Jim Plunkett

- I remember one July during training camp, when Bruce Davis, one of our offensive linemen, and his wife were expecting their first child. Of course, Bruce was very proud about having his first child on the way. He was telling Barnesy about it, to which Barnsey said, "Bruce, congratulations. By the way, when is the baby due?" Bruce said, "September." In true Barnesy deadpan fashion, Jeff asked, "This September?"

- Jeff is from California, and he knows the area very well. During training camp, we had a day off, and one of our young players wanted to go visit his relatives in Salinas, which is about 50 miles from Oakland. The guy asked Barnesy, "Where's Salinas?" Barnesy replied, "I don't know. I don't bother him, he don't bother me."

> • One day, right after I joined the Raiders, we were being pounded with a cold thunderstorm. It was wintertime, and it was getting dark early. We went inside after practice soaked to the gills, but we couldn't change clothes because the power had gone out. We couldn't shower or anything, because we couldn't see. Most of the guys took off their shoulder pads and helmets and took their stuff to their cars so they could just shower at home and bring everything back the next day. Barnesy was going around, asking for a ride home, because, since the power was out, he was afraid his car wouldn't start.

FRED BILETNIKOFF

Fred Biletnikoff and I played together during 1965-66. In fact, I threw Fred his first completion, his first touchdown, and his first dropped pass as a Raider. He was still with Oakland when I came back as an assistant coach in 1972. When I became head coach before the 1979 season I cut him. Actually, in this case "cut" sounds harsh because that's not exactly the case. Releasing him was largely his choice. Chances were that he wasn't going to make the team. He had been there a long time, and it was time to move on. However, he wanted to play one more year. He ended up playing for one of our former coaches, Joe Scannella, up in Canada for a year. Nevertheless, I guess you could say we went the whole cycle together.

Carry Me Home

Fred is a Hall of Famer in every sense. He was one of the greatest receivers of all time. It was my privilege to play with him when he was a rookie. I mentioned that I threw him his first dropped pass as a Raider. During that year, he dropped more than he probably dropped in his entire lifetime.

Fred Biletnikoff shows part of the reason why he's in the Pro Football Hall of Fame. *Photo courtesy of the Oakland Raiders.*

I carried him home when he damaged his knee in a game trying to block against San Diego. Blocking wasn't his forte. So we carried him home. In those days, if a guy hurt his knee, he came home with the team, made it through the night, and came to the training room the next day to have it checked out. We carried him up the stairs at this apartment and delivered him to his doorstep, where his wife was waiting. She wasn't very happy, so we just left him there and went home. He ended up having surgery on that knee, but fortunately it did not destroy the rest of his career.

Sign Right Here, Son

The Raiders drafted Fred out of Florida State. He actually signed his contract on the field right after Florida State had played in a bowl game. Al Davis was standing there, Fred was signing, and someone from one of the NFL teams was there trying to get him not to sign. It was like a circus out there. I'm not sure who drafted Fred from the NFL, but I know that Al was determined to sign him. Thank God he did.

Football Wedding

Fred got married under the goalpost that year. Not right after that game—obviously, he had already showered and shaved—but he did get married under the goalpost. I have no idea why. He took so much crap when he got to training camp that year from the veterans about the wedding under the goalpost. Fred had a good sense of humor, but after a while he reached his limit. He told everybody to shove off.

Getting Rid of the Jitters

Fred was so intense that he would throw up before each game. I don't know if he still does as a coach. He would throw up, and we could hear him in the bathroom. He looked like hell bent over, but then he would go out and play like a million dollars. He was that kind of guy.

Mentor

In 1972, the Raiders drafted Mike Siani in the first round and Cliff Branch in the fourth round. Out of three receivers, Fred was the only veteran. He was a mentor to those guys as far as his work ethnic. He would stay after practice and walk through routes. It helped the younger guys just to see Fred and to see what made him the player that he was.

I was a young coach in those days, so it also helped me out in coaching the receivers. Just being able to watch Fred work and try to teach the other kids was neat to see. He still had some things to learn about the philosophy of the game. He knew how to run routes, but he needed to know the overall picture. He needed to understand the big picture as to why he was doing what he was doing and why everybody else was doing what they were doing.

He did that—he learned and he paid his dues. He coached high school, junior college, and for the USFL before finally getting a job with the Raiders. He is doing quite well as a wide receiver coach. He certainly has left a great legacy with the Raiders.

DANNY BIRDWELL

If anything good happened in 1962—the year the Raiders finished 1-13—it would be that they drafted and signed Dan Birdwell out of Houston University. He ended up playing defensive line, but when the Raiders first drafted him he was a linebacker. He wasn't a real big guy for a defensive lineman, but he had good size for a linebacker, weighing about 235 pounds. He never was what you would call a heavyweight. I don't know that he ever weighed more than 250 pounds.

The "Birdman" or "Birdie," as we called him, was one of the most likeable guys you would want to meet. He was not very attractive like an Adonis, but he was well-built. He had so much natural strength that it was almost frightening. I don't think even he knew his own strength. It really didn't come out that much in 1962 because the team was so bad. We had many new faces. Danny's strength finally shone in 1963, when Al Davis came and we put Danny at defense.

Instead of just trying to play the old fashioned 4-3 defense that every-body played for so many years, AFL teams experimented with some things—overs-and-unders and where the defensive end is out on the tight end or outside the tight end. It wasn't until the Raiders perfected that defense that Danny finally started to flourish.

Heart of Gold

Danny had a heart of gold. I remember one time during training camp he came into my room and visited for a while. He asked if he could borrow a dollar. I guess he didn't have any money at all, so I loaned him a dollar. I later found out that right before asking me for a dollar, he had just loaned his last one to somebody else—or just gave it to him. That's the kind of guy that he was.

Lunchtime Ritual

Training camp, especially two-a-days, in hot Santa Rosa, was tiring. Between practices, most guys would go to lunch and then come back and relax a little bit, eventually sacking out. Many of the guys liked to watch the soap opera *Days of Our Lives*.

It was commonplace for some guys to grab some lunch, watch a soap opera at 12:30, and then take a little nap at 1:00. Then everyone would get up, go get taped, and be ready to practice again at 3:00. Guys would talk about the soaps around the circle. I mean here are a bunch of masculine guys who perceive themselves as macho types in the macho world of pro football, sitting there in the circle, stretching and talking about this soap—who was doing what and with whom, or whatever. I have to laugh when I say that because it's somewhat comical to think about. That even continued when I was coaching. So every generation used to do that. It was a ritual.

However, Danny's energy was endless. One day I had to go do something. As I was walking back to my room, I looked over and there was Danny, or at least part of Danny. I saw a car with some legs sticking out from underneath. Danny was working on his car in the hot sun, between practices, trying to fix something. He didn't seem to mind it. The engine might have been hot, but he didn't care.

Pain? What Pain?

Danny had a threshold of pain I've never known in my life. It ended up shortening his career because he hurt his knee and it required surgery. In those days, they'd put the leg in a huge cast—from the ankle to the hip—instead of the walking casts that doctors have nowadays. Obviously, they opened you up in those days for every type of knee surgery. Even if it was just the cartilage, the patient wound up with a huge scar. Also, the rehab was much different than it is today.

During the latter part of Danny's career, he was involved in some service stations. He would be working the service station in his cast, hobbling around. Pain was not an issue with Danny, but he got so tired of wearing the cast that he took it off himself. He didn't wait for the doctor to tell him when it was time. The doctors, the training staff, everybody, felt that move shortened his career. His last year was 1969.

Don't Tread on Me

Practicing with Danny was a treat. I remember in 1963, Al was trying to find a place for him, so he moved Danny to offense at second-team center during training camp. I was running with the second team when I came off my illness. His feet were on top of somebody else's on nearly every play.

He was like a bull in a china shop. He would get in the huddle and step on the guard's feet. He'd get up to the line of scrimmage, snap the ball, and then step on my feet as I was trying to get back in a pass drop. It was continuous. We always watched out for Birdie.

When they moved him back to defense that same year, we were lining up in practice, getting ready to run a play against our defense when we started to hear, "Ooh," "Ouch," "Ooh." We looked at the defense's huddle, and there he was, stepping on feet. Players had to be ready for Birdie, because he likely was going to step on a guy's foot.

Knockout

Danny had one speed and one speed only . . . full throttle. Oftentimes during practice, he lined up against the tight end. Billy Cannon was playing tight end at this time, so the two would line up against each other. At the snap of the ball, Danny would slap Billy across the helmet. In those days that was legal; it was just a head slap. That was part of Danny's charge up the field. We were just simulating this day, so Billy was not happy with Danny.

Billy said, "Birdie, don't do that. Don't slap me in the head."

"OK, OK."

They lined up, ran the play, and everything was fine. We came out of the huddle next time and lined up. The ball was snapped and *WHACK!* Birdie slapped Billy right across the helmet. Billy yelled at him again, and Birdie said, "Oh, you forgot to tell me not to."

During the season—I don't remember who we were playing—Birdie lined up across from the tight end, and at the snap of the ball, he head-slapped the tight end. The quarterback went back to pass, the tight end took four or five steps, slowed down, and then just fell. It was the funniest thing I had ever seen, but it wasn't so funny for that tight end, who lay on the ground for a while.

On film, though, it was hilarious. Birdie hit this poor tight end so hard that it was enough to daze him and knock him down. The guy didn't fall until he was about five yards up the field. It was a delayed-reaction knockout punch, I guess.

We Can Come Back and Win This!

During a preseason game in 1962 against the Broncos, we were getting our heads handed to us. (I wasn't on the team that year because I was rehabbing from my illness.) The Raiders were down by 35 points and were getting ready to receive another kickoff. Birdwell was on the kickoff coverage team. As usual, Danny was going where he was told, without questioning it. He would just get back there, laugh and have a good time. He had fun.

He got in the huddle before the kickoff and said, "Six quickies and we've got them!" I truly believe that Danny thought that it could be done. Regardless, he was going to go 100 percent, and the other guys better either go all out or look out, because Birdie's coming.

Farewell, Birdie

By the time I got back to the Raiders as an assistant coach in 1972, Danny's career had been finished for three years. When you take off your own cast, you don't rehab too well.

I didn't see him much when I was assistant coach. He was living in Fremont for a while and then he moved down to Southern California. I don't know why he moved there. I know that he married his second wife, who was a practicing nurse. We kind of lost track of Danny.

In 1979, Birdie died. Just like that. It was the strangest thing. A bunch of us flew down for the services—Al Davis; Ollie Spencer, who coached and played with the Raiders and Birdie in 1963; some of the other coaches; staff and players; and me.

He had written all of his kids a warm, touching letter, telling them how much he loved them. Then he lay down on the couch and died. The cause was unknown. It's surprising because Dan's father had died in a similar fashion. Maybe he lived so hard that it was just over for him. We miss him, because Danny was one of the most remarkable guys in the history of the Raiders franchise.

GEORGE BLANDA

In 1960, when the American Football League first started, I was a quarterback for the Raiders, and the quarterback for the Houston Oilers was a guy named George Blanda. George had already been in professional football for 10 years at that point. Many people don't realize or aren't aware that he started with the Chicago Bears in 1949. Sid Luckman was the Bears' main quarterback, so George was a linebacker and placekicker. When the AFL started, he became Houston's tough and tenacious veteran quarterback. He joined the Raiders through a trade in 1967 and played until 1975.

I don't think I have ever met anybody as competitive as George. He probably felt into his sixties that he could go out and kick a field goal, at least one, in the NFL. Then they could cart him off the field. Maybe that's the way that we should all go: one more play and we're outta here.

George had a phenomenal year in 1970, when he brought the Raiders from behind on several occasions. He did it again in 1971. Even in 1972, my first year as a coach with the Raiders, he would come in on occasion, get a quick touchdown, and then leave the game. He was just remarkable.

He always had certain plays in mind if he was called upon to go in as quarterback. He wasn't concerned with the entire game plan. He was concerned with maybe one drive, and he was remarkably successful when he did it. In those days, quarterbacks called their own plays, so George would take what he thought were the best plays and utilize them. He then would just march the team right down the field.

George was the kind of guy who went for the jugular. He would not hesitate. If the other team was down, he'd go for the jugular; if the other team was up, he'd go for the jugular. He didn't waste any time.

Whether it was on the field, off the field, on the golf course, playing cards, whatever, George was one of the most competitive—if not *the* most competitive—guy I've ever met. That's what makes George go. He's fun to be around because of his competitive nature. I wouldn't want to be around him if he were mad at me, but he certainly is fun when you are both on the same side.

The only sad thing about George's career is that he was about one year too early in his retirement. I don't know that he really wanted to retire, but the organization felt it was time. Ironically, the season after George retired, the Raiders won Super Bowl XI. Earl Mann was the kicker at the time, and he came in and helped us win a Super Bowl. It would have been nice to see George finish his career as a Super Bowl kicker, but I guess it just wasn't meant to be.

CLIFF BRANCH

The Raiders drafted Cliff Branch in 1972 in the fourth round. That was a great year for the draft. Mike Siani was a first-rounder from Villanova. Second round was John Villa from USC, an offensive lineman, who ended up starting for many years. There were two fourth-round picks—Dave Dalby and Cliff. Both of them had outstanding careers. Both of them were involved in three Super Bowl victories. Not many people can say that.

Cliff was the fastest receiver—fastest football player—that I have ever been around. I say football player because we brought guys into camp who could fly like trackmen, but they couldn't play football. Cliff was a football player who could run like a trackman. Actually, he couldn't come to the rookie mini-camp because he was on the track team at Colorado. So I was sent, as a first-year coach, to spend a week with him in Colorado. I learned that he was a delightful guy—he still is to this day. I also met his puppy, Raider, that Cliff named because he had been drafted by Oakland.

I don't know if Cliff has ever grown up. He loves to have fun and always has a smile on his face. During that week in Colorado, I introduced him to the rookie book and walked him through some routes. He couldn't run any routes, though, because of track. Al Davis flew in one time to watch him for half a day. I kept telling Al that there wasn't anything that Cliff could do that was going to excite Al that much, but he had to see Cliff in person to get a feel for him. Obviously, we all had to get a feel for him.

Cliff was a special guy. We knew that he could really run, catch the ball, and play the game of football. He tried out for the Olympics that year and came in fifth in the trials, missing out on going to the Olympics. He had a hamstring problem and that might have kept him from making the finals in the trials. However, he was eliminated and then we got him.

When we got him, he was recovering from a little strain, so we had to go easy with him for a while. Finally, we were able to run him, and we saw what kind of speed he had.

One thing I had to do was slow him down because he could glide faster than almost anybody could run on the field. He had another gear, which is the thing that separated him from everybody. He would be running and, all of a sudden, he would shift into the other gear. His separation was incredible. Everybody would stand there, amazed. We didn't know how tough he would be over the middle. He was not a big guy. He played at about 175 pounds, but he would catch the ball over the middle and make big plays.

Cliff started ahead of Mike Siani early in his rookie season in the season opener at Pittsburgh. During that game, though, he dropped some balls and suddenly had rookie-itis. Cliff was kind of like Fred Biletnikoff during his rookie year, except when Cliff dropped balls, he was behind everybody and the whole stadium saw it. Cliff became the third wide receiver when we

Cliff Branch (21) was the fastest football player I coached. *Photo courtesy of the Oakland Raiders.*

went to three wide receivers. In college, he played as a punt returner, kickoff returner, and wingback on a wing-formation set.

During his third year in the NFL, 1974, he finally became a starter again when Mike tore his Achilles during the preseason. Cliff was not looking forward to playing in front of the home crowd, because in his first two years, he had gotten some boos. He wasn't used to that. He said he would rather play only on the road. I told him that he couldn't do that. Well, he had such a great year he made the Pro Bowl. He then went on to be one of the most prolific guys for the Raiders——and one of the most prolific receivers in playoff history—playing in three Super Bowls. Only three Raiders—Gene Upshaw (24), Art Shell, and Dave Dalby (23 each)—have played in more postseason games than Cliff (22). (By the way, Ray Guy also played in 22 postseason games.) In terms of Raiders postseason records, Cliff also holds the record or is tied for the record in most pass receptions (73) and most yards gained (1,289) for a career and most pass receptions (nine) in a single game.

I still see Cliff occasionally in golf tournaments or at Raiders games. I think he still could play at his age, however old he is right now. I bet he could run about a 4.5 or 4.6 in the 40-meter dash. I asked him once what he would have run if we had ever timed him in the 40. He replied, "The way you time on my movement and not a starter's gun, probably 4.1 on grass."

That is fast, and that is Cliff Branch.

WILLIE BROWN

Willie Brown, who came out of Grambling, actually did not start with the Raiders. When I first ran into Willie, I literally ran into him. At that time, he was playing for the Denver Broncos and I was the quarterback for the Raiders. As is the case sometimes, I went back to pass but was forced to run, so I ran down the field and into Willie—or he ran into me. It's safe to say that he was trying to run into me more than I was trying to run into him.

I always kid Willie about his tackling in those days and how I ran over him. We laugh about it because neither of us is exactly sure what happened on that play. All I know is that I ran into Willie on the field in Mile High Stadium.

Willie was traded to the Raiders in 1967. That was the best move the Raiders had made in a long time, because Willie instantly became one of the dominating corners in the American Football League. He and Kent McCloughan came up to play tight coverage. They were both good-sized for cornerback standards in those days, and Willie was very physical.

A defensive back could do anything he wanted to a wide receiver in that era of football. He could cut the receiver. He could jam them. A defensive back couldn't hit them on the face or the mouth, but he could "accidentally" let his hand slip under the face mask into the throat area. That was one of Willie's favorite moves. The first thing he did off the line was hit his opponent in the upper chest, trying to knock the wind out of him with his hands. Once he did that, the receiver's pattern was finished. If the guy was really a tough receiver, a coach might have a linebacker cut the receiver at the line and then the defensive back would pick him up.

Willie was an outstanding cover man. He was beautiful to watch because he played with such ease. I remember watching him go against Warren Wells in practice, when Warren was still able to run. Willie would just glide through as if he knew exactly where Warren was going. That's how Willie played the game. That's why Willie is in the Hall of Fame.

When Willie was playing, the Raiders—and many teams do this—took their best defensive back (Willie) in one-on-one coverage and put him on the other team's best wide receiver. When we had Lester Hayes and Mike Haynes in the backfield, we didn't do that, because they both were outstanding cover guys, but with Willie, we used that strategy. Willie thrived on taking the best receiver. He was competitive and very proud of what he could do.

Willie's one of those guys who never was drafted. He didn't get a chance to play until the American Football League started. Wouldn't you know it, he ended up in the Hall of Fame, and rightfully so, because he had a good, long career.

Unfortunately, I never was Willie's head coach, but we did coach together. His last year playing was 1978, which was John Madden's last year as head coach. In 1979, we made Willie an assistant to our backfield coach. He was outstanding in the techniques and the drills. He was our secondary coach until 1988. He left for a few seasons to coach at Long Beach State, but now he's back with the Raiders.

He's still in a coaching capacity as the director of squad development. He takes care of players and their off-field achievements. I know he does bed check and rounds up players—he does a little bit of everything. Plus, he helps on the field and on the sideline during games.

In 1984, he became the third Raider enshrined in the Hall of Fame. As soon as he was eligible, he became a popular vote.

BILLY CANNON

Billy Cannon, who grew up in Mississippi and was the 1959 Heisman Trophy winner from Louisiana State University, was the first big name signed by the AFL, in 1960. In those days, Billy was a good size for a halfback, weighing about 200 pounds. Also, he ran under 10 seconds in the 100-yard dash (in those days, they were running yards, not meters). So Billy was fast for a big guy. There weren't many guys around who could run that fast at that size and play football. Most of the 9.9 to 9.8 sprinters were track guys.

Billy was probably the first football player of any notoriety to lift weights in college. He was kind of the forerunner of lifting weights and playing football. The old-fashioned thinking in those days was that you should not lift too many weights if you're a skill player: running back, wide receiver, quarterback, etc. Lifting weights was crude then. They didn't have the equipment that they have today or trainers who knew what they were doing regarding weights. The big men or the linemen were the ones who lifted weights.

Billy had the advantage of knowing a young guy named Alvin Roy, who was a weightlifting coach and later became a weightlifting guru in the NFL. Alvin had Billy lifting weights in college, which gave Billy tremendous strength that showed on the football field.

There Are Heroes and There Are Legends . . .

There is a line in the movie *The Sandlot* where the Babe Ruth character says something to the effect of, "Heroes get remembered, but legends never die."

Billy was a legend in the state of Louisiana and in the whole South. In fact, he still is a legend. I think the thing that probably won the Heisman for

The Players

Billy Cannon (33) was a legend in the South and a heck of a football player for the Raiders. *Photo courtesy of the Oakland Raiders.*

him happened on Halloween night in 1959. With No. 1 LSU trailing No. 3 Ole Miss 3-0 late in the game, Billy had a remarkable 89-yard punt return for a touchdown. A couple of months later, Billy won the Heisman.

That play became the most famous in LSU history and one of the most famous in the history of the Southeastern Conference.

They even had a song about Billy's touchdown run. For many years on Halloween night, radio stations in Baton Rouge played that song. Sportswriter Frank DeFord wrote a book, which inspired a movie with the same title, *Everybody's All-American.* The movie starred Dennis Quaid and Jessica Lange. The story was fictitious, but it was based on Billy's life. It was a story of a young kid out of nowhere who went to a major college, became an All-American, and fell in love with a Southern belle. It paralleled Billy's career through high school, college, and into the pros. It was a good movie.

I mention that because it's true how heroes are born and legends are made. People write songs and books about them and feature them in movies. That is how legends are treated down in the good old South.

A Great Asset

The Los Angeles Rams of the NFL and the Houston Oilers in the new AFL drafted Billy in 1960. He committed to the Rams, but then signed with the Oilers. There was a court battle, but obviously he won and was allowed to play for Houston.

The AFL had many big names: George Blanda was playing; Babe Parilli came down from Canada; Lenny Dawson got a chance to play, but he didn't come in the league until 1962, when he became a free agent and signed with the Dallas Texans. However, Billy was the first real rookie superstar who came into the AFL. It gave the AFL some credibility—not much, but a little—because nobody thought this league was going to make it.

Billy had a good rookie year in the AFL. One thing he was doing that he didn't do much at LSU was catching the ball. He had the ability, being the powerful guy he was. He continued to lift weights. In his first couple of years in the AFL, he was one of the league's foremost running backs. The Houston Oilers won the AFL championship for the first two years, 1960 and 1961.

In 1964, Billy was on the trading block. As players, we didn't know about it. We were all playing ball. Al Davis was in his second year as the Raiders' head coach, and we played a preseason game against the Oilers in Las Vegas. Both teams stayed at the Desert Inn. Both teams were in the lobby—or at the blackjack table—before the game. Billy knew that he was being shopped around, and I think he really wanted to come to Oakland. He played like a man possessed that night.

We were all impressed with him, not knowing that he was going to be traded shortly thereafter. This was something that was kept a secret in those days; not everything was publicized. There were still some things that were secret and left that way. People didn't nose around as they do now.

Billy was traded to the Raiders that year. He fit in, yet he didn't fit in. He was a cross between a fullback and a halfback. We had Clemon Daniels, who was a tremendous halfback for us, and Alan Miller had been our fullback. Billy started playing fullback for us. His advantage was his ability to catch the football. He had great hands. Obviously, his speed down the field was a weapon, too.

After Billy's first year with us, Al decided that he would move Billy to tight end. Billy was a tremendous competitor, and by this time he had grown in size. Not the size of the guys today playing tight end, but he was up there in weight. I'm not so sure how much he weighed, but I would imagine he was in the neighborhood of 225-230 pounds, maybe even more. At 6-foot-1, he was not tall, but he was big enough. Regardless, he could run, and he was deceptive when he ran. He was very powerful and strong.

Over the next few years, Billy set a precedent for what tight ends were going to be in the future, because he was one who could go deep. Indeed, he could get down the field. He wasn't the kind of tight end who just blocked, caught little short passes, and then ran over people to get a long gain. He was the guy who could catch the ball down the field—30, 40, 50 yards—and then go in for the score.

I remember one game when we were playing Kansas City and I called a deep corner route to Billy. He caught the ball about 40 yards down the field, turned the corner, and outran everybody to the end zone, about 70 yards.

Dr. Cannon

Billy played with the Raiders during 1964-69, which included their Super Bowl II year of 1967. He also played in the 1969 AFL All-Star Game.

During the off-season, unbeknownst to most of us, Billy went to school. He ended up going to dental school. People didn't realize he was doing that at the time. I didn't know it and I considered myself a good friend of his. I finally found out that he was going to dental school and was getting ready to do graduate work and become an orthodontist.

In 1970, the Raiders released him. The Chiefs picked him up as a tight end. Ironically, I was with the Chiefs at the time. We roomed together and became even closer. Even though he was aging, Billy was still a force. He was starting to show some of the wear and tear of his career. He wasn't as durable as he had been in the past, but he still was effective and still able to do a few things.

That was about the time that he started winding down his commitment to the game of football. He was finishing orthodontist school and getting ready to go into that field. Today, he is a practicing orthodontist in Baton Rouge. I haven't talked to Billy for a while, but he is doing what he wanted to do.

Billy is a very smart, bright individual. He's also very proud and a stubborn Southerner. He loved the game and the camaraderie. He had a mission, and he accomplished his goals. The only sad thing was he never became a Super Bowl champion, although he did get to play in Super Bowl II. He was one of the 18 guys who made it through the AFL's 10-year existence. Considering the uncertainty of the league and the financial problems that some of the teams had in the early years, being one of the 18 who made it is something to be proud of.

If Billy left a legacy, it was proving that a skill player could lift weights and still be a good player. He proved that a tight end could go down the field and catch the ball deep. He also proved that a player could go to school in the off-season and become a professional—that there is life after football. His legacy was that he was one of the first guys to be able to do all of those things. I think because of that, his career was remarkable.

Billy is one of the most memorable guys in the history of the Oakland Raiders. He always was a Raider. Even though he started with the Oilers and ended with the Chiefs, to those of us in the organization he always will be a Raider.

DAVID CASPER

After Raymond Chester was traded in 1972, we needed a top tight end. We picked David "The Ghost" Casper in the second round of the 1974 draft out of Notre Dame. The second round is where we took a lot of guys that we felt were maybe not true second-rounders, but they had some ability that we thought that we would be able to bring out on the football field. Some of the best Raiders, whether that idea held true or not, came out of the second round. David certainly was a great second-round selection.

David was a tackle for one year at Notre Dame before becoming a tight end. When he came to us in one of the rookie camps, he weighed about 260 pounds. In one of the sessions, John Madden put David in as a lineman. David came back to the next rookie camp weighing about 235 pounds. He had lost a few pounds and was more suited for the tight end position.

David was never a real speed guy, but he was deceptive. He had quick feet. He could come out of a cut as well as any tight end I've ever seen. He was a very quick learner. I wasn't going to show him how to play tight end; I was going to show him how to play the game. He had all the techniques. He was the best total blocking tight end I have ever been around. If you had wanted to make a film to teach techniques, David would have been a good guy to use as an example. Although he had funny-looking arms—they were a little crooked—he was explosive. When he ran a route, he could come out of it so quickly that he would get the edge on a defensive back.

I think the most famous play he made was against the Baltimore Colts in the 1977 playoffs. It was a double-overtime game where he made a great catch. Not too many tight ends—and not too many receivers—could have made that catch. It's still known as "Ghost to the Post." On this particular play, David watched the ball sail from over his left shoulder to over his right shoulder. He turned his head, reached up, and made a spectacular catch. Most players would have stumbled on that play—not the "Ghost."

The "Ghost," Dave Casper. *Photo courtesy of Tom Flores.*

David's other big play was the "Holy Roller" play in San Diego. Kenny Stabler went back to pass on fourth down, and the ball came loose. Pete Banaszak tried to pick it up, but kicked it down to about the five-yard line. Ghost tried to pick it up, but kicked it into the end zone. He then fell on it for a touchdown, and we won the game. The NFL changed the rules because of that, but the Ghost was part of that.

David was so bright that he got bored very easily. And he didn't like to go to meetings because he already knew what was going to happen. However, one time he begged me to not make him go to the meetings.

"Please, I'll do anything. I'll go watch tapes in the other room," he said. I replied, "Now, David, if I have to go, you have to go." So he went.

He liked to doodle—draw little pictures. One time when I had the guys in a meeting when I was an assistant coach, David was drawing. I asked him to repeat what I had just said and he did—verbatim. I asked him another question, and he answered that correctly, too. Doodling was just his way of occupying his mind so he wouldn't go bananas. When David got bored, he would get in trouble.

I remember the night in 1980 when we traded David. He was not a happy camper, and we couldn't even find him to tell him that we had traded him. We finally found him about 11:00 at night. He came into my office and I told him that we traded him to Houston. I wished him good luck and told him that hopefully he would straighten out his professional and personal life. He did straighten it out, and he made the Pro Bowl that year. We brought him back to the Raiders in 1984 when we were in L.A., just for half of a season.

David lived in Minnesota, but now he's back in the Bay area. He goes to a lot of the Raiders games. He has two daughters, who are young women now, and a son, Andy, who's in high school playing football. I don't think he is a tight end, so I don't think he'll carry on the traditions, but he's another "Ghost" who can play. This Ghost might not go to the post, but just like his dad, he's a wonderful kid.

BOBBY CHANDLER

My first year coaching in the National Football League was 1971. I was an interim coach with the Bills. The night before training camp, head coach John Rauch had a run-in with owner Ralph Wilson, who demanded some apologies because John had criticized some of the veterans. John refused to apologize, so he quit! I was called to run the offense because I knew it. It was the same one I had run as a player in Oakland for years.

Offensively, that team was loaded. Haven Moses was there. Marlin Briscoe was coming off a great year at wide receiver. O. J. Simpson was in the backfield, and they had just drafted J. D. Hill in the first round and Bobby Chandler in the seventh round. We had some weapons.

Obviously, J. D., Marlin, and Haven were going to make the team. The Bills were keeping only three wide receivers. In our staff meeting I said, "This guy Chandler is really pretty good. He's doing everything. He's running routes, he's catching the ball, and he's got excellent speed."

Still, they said we couldn't afford to keep four wide receivers, only three. The squads were smaller in those days. Unfortunately for J. D., he injured his knee in a preseason game and had to have surgery, so Bobby made the team. Once he made it, he became a mainstay in Buffalo for several years.

In 1980, when I was back with the Raiders, we traded to get Bobby. He had a great year for us, making some terrific catches and leading the team in receiving yards with 786. He was a complete player and a great team player.

Sadly, Bobby was diagnosed with cancer and died very quickly in 1995.

I will always remember sitting in the locker room after we had beaten the Philadelphia Eagles in Super Bowl XV. Al Davis and I were reflecting on the season. Most everybody was gone from the locker room. Bobby stuck his head in the room, with tears in his eyes, and said, "Thanks. Thank you very much." Then he walked out. It was another one of those warm, fuzzy moments that I will never forget.

RAYMOND CHESTER

The Raiders have always had good tight ends. When I played for the Raiders, we had Billy Cannon. Then, when I came back as an assistant coach, we had Raymond Chester, who had been drafted in the first round in 1970. Raymond was chiseled and powerful. He had great speed for a big guy. He probably was one of the best man-on-man blockers because of his sheer strength. Raymond had a wonderful career, and he was an outstanding leader.

He could catch the ball and then run over or run right by people. So we took full advantage of his skills. We had to utilize Raymond because he was such a force. He made the Pro Bowl as a tight end with us all three of his early years, 1970-72, and again when he came back to us in 1979. That year we had to use two tight ends—Chester and Dave Casper—because they were our best players. We became the only team in the history of the NFL to have both tight ends in the Pro Bowl in the same year.

In 1973, against some of our wishes—I wasn't too thrilled about it and I'm not sure John Madden was either—Raymond was traded to the Baltimore Colts for Bubba Smith. Al Davis always liked Bubba because Bubba was a great defensive end at one time. Coming back from a knee injury, though, he never really regained the playing ability that he had before the injury. He was good and he helped us win some games, but that was a big trade. We missed Raymond.

Raymond came back in 1978, and, as I said, in 1979 he went back to the Pro Bowl. In 1980, when we traded David, Raymond became the lone starting tight end and helped us go to a Super Bowl. He was a big part of a magical year for us.

If you could sculpt a body for a tight end, Raymond would be the model. If you were going to take a guy for speed, Raymond would be the guy. If you were going to take a guy for power, Raymond would be the guy. He was not very fluid—Raymond was a little stiff when he ran—but he was still such a tremendous specimen. He would just overpower people at times. It was very deceiving, because he would be on you so fast and guys were not used to tight ends being able to run that fast.

Raymond Chester listens intently as I give him some last-minute instructions in 1979. *Photo courtesy of Tom Flores.*

He was one of the great leaders for our team, particularly that Super Bowl year. He was a veteran, and he was one of the ones that held the team together when we started shaky that season. He helped us keep the sanity in place. He caught a big touchdown pass in the AFC Championship Game against San Diego.

Raymond had a great career and was able to finish it in Oakland. He now lives there and is a very prominent businessman in the community and a loyal Raiders supporter.

TODD CHRISTENSEN

Todd Christensen was a running back and tight end out of Brigham Young University. He played with the Raiders during 1979-88. Todd was an interesting study. I didn't know that much about him. We studied him during the draft, but I believe the Dallas Cowboys took him in the second round. I don't exactly know what happened to him there. I'm not sure whether they wanted to make him a tight end, but, for whatever reason, they released him.

The New York Giants picked him up for a very short amount of time. As we sometimes say in sports, he was with the Giants long enough to get a cup of coffee. Then, all of a sudden, he showed up in our camp. Al Davis always liked players like that. It didn't cost us anything. We didn't have to trade for him or give him a signing bonus. All we had to do was sign him. He was a free agent—no restrictions.

Todd wasn't a pure fullback. He probably would have been a better halfback. At that time, though, we didn't use the halfback. As we found out more and more about him, we realized he would have been good at the halfback—moving around from side to side and lining up on all different types of sets. Without question, Todd was a great receiving tight end. He could do it all at that position.

In 1979, we used Todd out of the backfield. We didn't use him at tight end. Understand that he would have been our fourth-string tight end behind David Casper, Raymond Chester, and young Derrick Ramsey. Really, how often is a fourth-string guy going to play behind that group? Talk about talented guys all sitting in one position, so we had to use him in some other way.

We used him on special plays out of the backfield as a fullback, in the play-action going down the field. He could definitely run. He had great speed for his size and he caught the ball fearlessly in any kind of traffic. He was tenacious.

That was my first year coaching and I felt we had to make an adjustment to get our best players on the field. In our slot formation we treated the closed-in side as the backside, with the halfback and the tight end running combination routes. The other side was a regular side, with the tight end and wide receiver. So for tight ends we had David on one side and Raymond on the other. Occasionally, we'd put Todd in a regular set. The first couple of years he was with us, we tried to utilize his talent as a receiver as best as we could.

Todd was primarily a special-teams guy and he was very good at it. He was our snapper on punts. He could zip the ball. He was on the coverage teams, the return teams, and the punt team. He was an all-around athlete. Even when he became a starter on offense, including Super Bowl XV, he was the punt snapper. We tried to utilize everything that he could do, and he eventually worked his way up to being a starter.

In 1980, we traded David, but that left us with Raymond and Derrick as our top two tight ends. Since that made Todd our third tight end, we were using him more. His first season to get going was 1981, when we tried to isolate him on guys and tried to work him down the field.

Patience Pays Off

Todd was a team guy, and he worked hard to become a better player. He did everything that we asked him to do. That's not always easy for a player who thinks he should be playing, but Todd was patient. I think he really felt in time he would get his opportunity and then he would take advantage of it.

In 1982, his time came. He became an active player in our offense as a tight end. Not in the backfield, but as a tight end. He worked on his blocking skills and he was adequate in that department, but he really excelled as a receiver down the field.

From that point forward, he had big years. He was in five Pro Bowls. He holds the second- and third-place spots for Raiders all-time receiving in a season. In 1986, he caught 95 passes, three more than he caught in 1983. In fact, three times during the 1986 season, he caught 11 passes in one game. He was, without question, one of the more prolific tight ends in the history of the Raiders.

Whenever we were designing a game plan and I was working on the red zone passes, I tried to have at least three ways that we could get the ball to Todd. He certainly could catch the ball in the red zone. As I mentioned earlier, he was a fearless receiver, diving and making one-handed catches.

Todd was one of those guys with tremendous burst out of his route to the ball. He was one of those guys who, when the ball was in the air, had another little spurt to go. He could catch it with his hands or his body—whatever he had to. He did it all in that respect.

Philosopher

Todd was a philosophical type of guy. He read poetry and studied the famous philosophers. He prided himself on being able to quote poets and great thinkers. Henry David Thoreau was one of his favorites, or at least the one I remember him using the most.

We were practicing one day and I was trying to get the guys to the huddle to call a play. Todd was waxing profound on some concept. He said some blah-blah-blah quote and then attributed Thoreau. I just looked at him and said, "Get your @#&%ing ass in the huddle," and attributed that to Tennessee Williams.

Todd looked at me and said "Ah, touché," with a big smile. Everybody chuckled a little, but I don't think most of the guys understood it. They didn't know who in hell Thoreau was. Fortunately, I knew who he was, but

I'll admit that I didn't know what he did. Obviously, Todd knew, but I knew who Tennessee Williams was.

My experience over the years has been that some of the great, outstanding, unique players also were very bright. They knew exactly what was going on, to a point where they would get bored. Guys like David, Ted Hendricks, and Todd knew everything that was happening on the field. They were quick learners and they retained information. I didn't have to keep repeating it to them. Because I often had to repeat for the other players, those guys like Todd got bored. And when they got bored, they became a little bit of a nuisance.

They'd do little things to let me know that they were bored. Their actions weren't detrimental to the team or to the locker room, but sometimes when a coach is tired and he's been working hard, he still has to find ways to entertain these guys.

Special Plays for a Special Player

We were more creative with Todd than we were with some of the other guys, because he could do different things. If a coach is smart enough—and I always considered myself to have a good football mind—he learns how to take advantage of special talents.

For instance, we had special plays for David, Raymond, and Billy Cannon. Todd could do certain things that those other guys couldn't do and vice versa. That's just the way it is.

Todd thrived on finding out what special play we had for him. When we handed out the game plans each week, the first thing he did was look at the specials. We always had specials—big-time yardage plays, red-zone plays, third-down plays—and he always looked for them because he knew that there were going to be two to four new ideas that week. He loved being a part of that.

I always will remember him thumbing through the game plan to see what was new and what the challenges were going to be. He always rose to the challenge. He was an outstanding player for the Raiders and helped us win a Super Bowl.

A Real Job

It's fun for a coach to watch players grow up. Some of them grow up under your wing, and some don't grow up until they're gone. Todd was mature. Most of our players were kids in adult bodies. Todd wasn't as childish as some of our other guys were. Some of our guys were just kids, and they loved to play. Todd loved to play the game, and he liked to excel, but he took it seriously. He knew that one day he would have to find a "real job."

When the team was in Los Angeles, he got a chance to do some preliminary work on what he thought might be his future—radio and television. After spending some time with NBC, Todd is now doing quite well with ESPN as a college football analyst.

Todd has always been very knowledgeable and loquacious. He handles the English language very well—in fact, sometimes too well. His explanations are sometimes difficult to understand. I don't know that the average fan understands him all the time.

He would use some words that I didn't understand. (Of course, I never let him know that.) He used a word one time when we were talking and I had to look it up in the dictionary after he left my office.

The fun part about these guys growing up and being successful after they leave is that as a coach you've been an important part of their lives. They've helped you and you've helped them and together you won a Super Bowl.

At one time, Todd thought about getting into coaching. He approached me when I was in Seattle about the possibility of coaching with the Seahawks. I don't know if it would have worked. Certainly, staying with television has been great for him.

It's fun to watch BYU play now and see a guy named Toby Christensen. That's little Toby, whom I remember coming to practices on Saturdays. On Saturdays, we allowed the players to bring their kids if they wanted to. The kids were allowed on the field, and we'd have somebody corral them, keeping them out of the way. Toby's no longer a tiny kid running around our field. Now he's at BYU catching passes. I don't know if he's the same caliber as Todd was, but if he's even close he should have a solid career at BYU. Who knows what will happen after college?

Regardless, Todd has given BYU a legacy. Even if the Raiders don't get his legacy, we certainly have some great memories of Todd Christensen.

DAN CONNERS

Dan Conners was a rookie in 1964 out of the University of Miami. He played with the Raiders through the 1974 season. Dan actually was a defensive tackle in college, but the Raiders made him stand up and play linebacker in the NFL.

Dan might have been the first one to start the tradition of playing a down lineman but not being as big or having the body of a down lineman. We stood him up to play linebacker. After we did that with Dan, we also did it with Monte Johnson and Matt Millen.

Dan was one of the smartest linebackers in the history of the Raiders franchise. Dan wasn't fast or strong, but he was quick. His biggest strength was his knowledge and his ability to be in the right place at the right time. He was there for an interception, a fumble, to cause a fumble—you name it, and Dan was there.

To opponents, he was a pain in the ass. He was great when I played with him, but when I was traded and had to play against him, he was a big pain because he was always making plays. That was Dan.

Dan won't go down in history as one of the great linebackers, but he will go down in the Raiders' history as one of the great playmakers.

John Madden talks strategy with Dan Conners (55) and George Atkinson (43) during a game in 1969. *Photo courtesy of the Oakland Raiders.*

CLEMON DANIELS

Clemon "Clem" Daniels, who played at Prairie View College in Texas, was one of the great runners in the 1960s. Clemon played with the Raiders during 1961-67. He ended up with the San Francisco 49ers in 1968. I don't know how good Clem was in college. In those days black schools were not scouted as much as they are today. Black players didn't have a lot of choices back then because the major colleges weren't looking to take that many black players. Many of the great players of that era went to black schools—Buck Buchanan, Willie Brown, Ernie Ladd, and Clem.

Clem originally signed with the Dallas Texans. I think he started out as a defensive back. They already had pretty good talent, so they released him.

Everyone in the AFL was improving except the poor old Oakland Raiders. In 1961, the Raiders signed two of their 30 draft choices. One of them was George Fleming, who was a running back and a kicker. He was a second-round choice out of Washington. He still has a Raiders record with a 54-yard field goal, which is unique in itself, because it was made at Candlestick Park and he was a straight-ahead kicker.

The other guy from the 1961 draft who signed was Bob Coolbaugh, out of Richmond, who was a 15th-round choice. We didn't have many new faces to give our club a boost. That's probably why we won only two games in 1961.

Fortunately for the Raiders, the Texans released Clem. I don't know if anybody in our organization knew exactly what they were doing, but somebody picked up Clem, which was a good choice. There were not a lot of good choices or smart moves made in those days, but that was a good one.

Put Him Through the Mill

I remember one of Clem's first days of practice. He was kind of quiet, just like any new rookie or new player from another team. Being from Texas and playing for the Texans, he was right there in Dallas, and everything was going well for him. All of the sudden, he's in Oakland, playing games across the Bay at Candlestick Park, and practicing at the Alameda Naval Base. I'm sure there was some culture shock.

On Clem's first day of practice he played fullback. I don't remember exactly what type of face bar he had, but I do remember that he got a big gash on his chin from blocking. They put him through the mill to find out if he could play or not. That's usually the way you did it with players in those days whom you didn't know much about. You found out first if they were tough, if they had any talent and if they had any intelligence, and then you found out if they could play. You gave them a chance to play if they had all of the other ingredients.

Clem had speed and size, and he showed that he had toughness. He was running at fullback and eventually ended up running at the halfback spot. He was not a full-time guy during practice in those years. He shared the duties with Wayne Crow, who was out of the University of California.

Clem did not make much of a contribution, although he did some things that were good. People didn't really get a chance to see all of his talents, because the offense was kind of limited and he was just a backup at that time.

Al Davis

Clem's second year in Oakland, 1962, was a disaster for the Raiders. I missed it because I had tuberculosis. I sat out the whole year. During the season, the Raiders fired their second coach, Marty Feldman, who had been hired about three games into the season the year before.

Red Conkright took over. He brought in some of his guys from Houston and all over the place. Clem still didn't get a chance to do much because the team was so bad. Really, no one shone because the team was so lousy. The Raiders won one game that year, the last game of the year against the Boston Patriots, who were in the running for the championship. Had Houston lost their last game, Boston would've been the champs in the Eastern division. Houston won, so Boston was out of it. At least our team did something that season.

After that season, Conkright was fired and Al Davis was hired as head coach and general manager. The one word about Al was that he was a great recruiter, and he could recognize talent. In 1963, Clem became the starting halfback.

Clem was unique in that he was big for a halfback. Cleveland's Jimmy Brown was a big halfback, but he was in a class by himself. I think Clem, at that point, was also close to being in a class by himself because he was a big back by most standards. He weighed about 215 pounds. He had great speed and a great ability to bounce outside. He was built very well. Most of all, he had terrific hands. He had a great ability to catch the ball on anything short or medium, but especially down the field on deep routes.

That's one thing that Davis liked to do, and the Raiders offense was geared for it—get the ball to the wideouts or get the ball to your halfbacks down the field. At that time, we didn't have a tight end who could get down the field. So instead of the tight end we put Clem down the field. Every week, Al tried to find more and different ways to get the ball into Clem's hands.

Clem was having a banner year. It was fun to watch a big guy develop that way and to be able to do the things that he did.

Humble Halfback

One of the reasons that I think Clem was unique in the history of Raiders football is because he established what the prototypical halfback should be for the Raiders. The Raider philosophy stayed that way for years and years. That is: a halfback for the Raiders should be able to run the ball inside, bounce to the outside, block adequately, and, above that, be able to catch the ball on screen passes or down the field. Clem could do all of those things with such effectiveness. Because of his outstanding season, Clem was the team's Player of the Year in 1963.

It's remarkable that Clem did all of this and still retained his humble personality. He didn't get big-headed. Of course, we weren't making a lot of money in those days, and we weren't on the front pages of the newspapers

Clem Davis was a big back with great speed. *Photo courtesy of the Oakland Raiders.*

all of the time. But Clem was a guy who was certainly a Raiders legend through the 1960s and the days of the AFL. He was one of the all-time best backs to come out of the AFL. He didn't have a long career, but it was a good career.

He stayed in Oakland after his playing career ended. He is a very successful businessman today. He still follows the Raiders and goes to the games with his family. He has always been a private person. You've never heard bad things about Clem. The uniqueness of him was that he was a classy guy in a very tough environment and always maintained it. He had a lot of success that he worked hard for. Obviously, he had enough intelligence, perseverance, and fortitude to go into the business world and be very successful. People think highly of him in the football world and in the business world in Oakland.

BEN DAVIDSON

Ben Davidson was a defensive lineman for the Raiders during 1964–71. He was a big, gangly, string-bean guy at 6-foot-7. He didn't start at the University of Washington, but he probably had not grown into his body yet. That was the case during his brief stint with the Washington Redskins before the Raiders picked him up. Once he started playing and getting experience, the better he got. He started making big plays, which happens sometimes when a player starts to mature.

Ben needed a team to take a chance on him and give him an opportunity. The Raiders were that team. We had patience because we needed players. On top of that, Al Davis always liked guys with size. Ben had size and speed, and he became an excellent pass rusher.

Ben probably is best remembered for two huge hits on quarterbacks. One was when he sacked New York's Joe Namath. In today's game, he would have been flagged for it because it was so late.

The other one was during a 1970 game against Kansas City, when he nailed Lenny Dawson, causing a big free-for-all. Chiefs receiver Otis Taylor put a retaliation hit on Ben, and all of that ended up costing the Chiefs the game. But that was Ben. He was always doing things of that nature.

Injuries

Ben was a neat guy with a raspy voice. He didn't always talk with the raspy voice, though. He had a normal voice when he joined the Raiders, but he was clotheslined right in the Adam's apple. (In those days, clotheslining was part of the game.) That caused him to go from talking normally to the raspy voice that became his trademark.

Although that injury didn't affect his career, one did a few years later. In 1972, we were playing a preseason game in Berkeley at the University of California, and Ben was chasing down a running back. Suddenly, he went down like a shot. Ben blew out his Achilles tendon, and that was the end of his career.

Ambassador

After Ben left football, he had bit parts in some movies. He was in the "Tastes great; less filling" Miller Lite commercials. He's owned some real estate. Good of Ben—a hard-nosed defensive lineman whom people would not have figured for a good businessman. Indeed, he has great business acumen.

If ever there was an ambassador for the Raiders, Ben had to be one of the best, because he would go anywhere, any time, and represent the organization. It didn't matter if he was paid a fee or just fed dinner; he was a great guy to promote the Raiders.

Not only was he a great ambassador for the Raiders, he was a great ambassador for professional football, period.

HEWRITT DIXON

Hewritt Dixon had been a tight end with Denver when we picked him up before the 1966 season. He was not very good as a tight end, but he was a talented football player. Hewritt had tremendous hands, and he was a 6-foot-2, 235-pound guy with excellent speed. So when the Raiders picked him up they made him a fullback. He had played fullback some, but not in the pros. I don't think Hewritt realized what kind of abilities he had. He was a very powerful guy and was deceptive with his speed, tremendous catching skills, and running skills. He could really punish somebody if he wanted to.

His coming-out game was when we were playing a doubleheader down in Anaheim Stadium. We were down by the goal line. I can't remember the exchange, but I do remember calling his play and saying something like, "Run their asses over." Hewritt got the ball, turned the corner, and used his big forearm to level some linebacker. It was beautiful to see this 235-pound man realize that he could run over people, instead of trying to go around them. He became dangerous when he had the ball. He was like a big truck. He would lower that shoulder and rip up on the defensive players. There couldn't have been too many guys who enjoyed tackling Hewritt. He is also the only running back I've ever seen penalized for using his forearm to level a defender.

He went on to become an outstanding football player for the Raiders, both as a running back, a blocking back, and as a receiver. He had a very good career.

RAY GUY

The Raiders drafted Ray Guy in the first round in 1973 out of Southern Mississippi—yes, Ray Guy, the punter. Who's going to draft a punter in the first round? To top it off, when the Raiders drafted Ray his left ankle was in a cast from an injury. So they not only drafted a punter in the first round, but they also drafted a punter who had a damaged ankle.

I am sure the rest of the league was wondering what we were doing, but the feeling in the draft room was that he would make the biggest impact of all the guys who were on the board. The Raiders have always had that philosophy in the first round. Who's going to make the most impact? Gene Upshaw was a first-round guy; Mike Haynes was a first-rounder whom we traded for; and Marcus Allen was a first-round guy.

In 1973, the thought was that a punter could make the biggest impact immediately. With a quarterback it could take a little while. Certain positions take a little bit longer to mature. However, Ray was an outstanding athlete. He could run, jump, throw the ball about 80 yards in the air, and even dunk a basketball. Because of his ability to throw, we made him our disaster quarterback.

As a punter, he was incredible. He could punt the ball out of sight. He would put on exhibitions sometimes. He'd get on a roll, and we'd have to get out the vaudeville hook to get him off the field.

Put Me In, Coach

I remember the first rookie camp that we had when Ray was drafted. He was a defensive back in college. He was about to go with the backs and receivers to run some one-on-one drills and cover drills. He was wearing a dark jersey just like the rest of the defensive backs.

Soon, Ray got on the field to cover somebody. We all just stared for a few seconds. We didn't know what to do. John Madden and Al Davis were watching from the side and both of them realized that they had to grab Ray off the field. John said, "Whoa, whoa, just wait a minute! You, get off the field, stand there and watch."

Not too long after that we put a red jersey on Ray. We let him learn some of the quarterback plays and how to take snaps. We made him a part of our practice. We tried to do things to keep him interested and utilize his great talent.

Hall of Fame

I don't understand why Ray's not in the Hall of Fame. It's incredible because there is one guy on that voting committee who says he will "never vote for a punter." That guy shouldn't even be allowed to vote. The Hall of Fame is for outstanding performers in football. The last time I checked, punters and kickers were a big part of professional football. Ray certainly was a big part of the Raiders' success.

Miracle Punt

In Super Bowl XVIII, right before the half, we were up 14-3, I think, and we were punting. Ray was standing on our 25-yard line and the ball was snapped way over his head. There isn't anybody I can think of who could have made this play. Nevertheless, Ray went up in the air—I don't know how high—and with one hand he grabbed the ball, came down without losing a stride, and punted the ball out-of-bounds inside the Redskins' 20-yard line.

That ball would have sailed over any other punter's head and the opponent would have had the ball inside the 20-yard line. Instead, Ray bailed us out in a huge way. It was the same game where Washington quarterback Joe Theismann threw the ball to our Jack Squirek; it hit him right in stride and he ran it back for a touchdown right before the half. I'm not sure if that is the same series or not, but Ray certainly got us out of the hole. It could have been a completely different game going into halftime had they been able to score. They certainly would have had great field position and a great opportunity to score.

I have a picture of Ray going up in the air for that ball hanging in my garage where I can see it every day and remember that play.

Super Team Competition

After Super Bowl XV, 10 of my guys and 10 of the Eagles were picked to go to Honolulu and perform in this Olympic-kind of competition—swimming, running, jumping, rowing, tug-of-war, etc. Ray was probably the best athlete there in running, jumping, swimming, and rowing. Ray could do it all.

Disaster Quarterback

The one time I can recall Ray being a little reluctant about what he was going to do was during a game in Chicago. This was when the Bears were really starting to become good. Our quarterback, Jim Plunkett, was already hurt that season, and then Marc Wilson went down. While Marc was in the locker room getting an X-ray, third-string quarterback David Humm blew out his knee. So I told Ray to get ready to go into the ballgame. He couldn't believe it.

I was trying to tell him what I wanted him to do, but I don't know how much attention he was paying to me. His eyes were focused on the tunnel. Suddenly, Marc came running out because he saw David get hurt on TV and he knew that Ray would have to go in. That was not a good game for Ray to make his NFL quarterbacking debut. Those Bears were coming hard. When Marc came out of the tunnel, Ray got this look of relief in his eyes.

We put Jim McMahon out of the game; they put David out of the game and out of football. This was not a good game for an inexperienced guy at

quarterback. Ray had taken a few snaps along the way, but nothing like this. Marc came back and went into the ballgame.

Don't get me wrong; Ray would have gone in. And we would have put him in. We would have protected him, and he would have executed to the best of his ability. I don't know how well he would have played, and I'm glad I didn't have to find out. He sat in on all the quarterback meetings, asked questions, took some notes, and practiced just so that he would be ready to execute if we got to that point. Luckily, we didn't.

WAYNE HAWKINS

Wayne Hawkins and I were teammates at the College of the Pacific. He was another original Raider in 1960. Wayne played tackle in college, but when he came to the Raiders, he was moved to guard. I didn't know if he could play guard because I didn't know if he could pull, but Wayne proved himself. He played all 10 years of the AFL's existence as a starter, missing very few games. He hurt his hip in 1970, and that was the end of his career.

Is He Dead?

Wayne was as solid a player as you'd ever want to see. He acted like our barometer. Wayne had a great attitude. During two-a-days—which seem to last forever—when everybody would be dying, we'd look at Wayne to see how he was doing. If he had a smile on his face, then we were OK. Now, if he didn't have a smile on his face, we knew things were bad.

In those days, we didn't have off-season conditioning programs. Guys came to camp to get in shape. During one of Al Davis' first practices in his early years as head coach, he put us through the grind, boy. It was almost as

I still do not know how Ray Guy made this incredible one-handed grab in Super Bowl XVIII. *Photo courtesy of the Oakland Raiders and the* St. Petersburg Times.

if he was setting the tempo for everybody. Wayne about died—at least that's how it looked.

Practice was over on this particular day and we were all in the locker room. We were showered and getting ready to go relax before we went out for a beer or two, before the meal and our evening meetings. All of a sudden, we realized that Wayne wasn't around. We looked out onto the field and there he was, still lying on the field. I thought he was dead. He was so wasted from the sprints and the workout that he couldn't get up. Finally, he got off the field, recovering later that night. The next day, he was not in shape yet, but at least he knew what to expect. He didn't suffer as much, and from then on he knew the routine and made sure he was in some kind of shape when he came to camp.

Three Amigos

Wayne and I have been dear friends all our lives. We were in each other's weddings. To this day, we are still the best of friends, but I don't see him as much as I used to. Wayne was one of those guys who always had a good sense of humor.

Wayne, Jim Otto, and I used to buddy around together in those early Raiders years. We were part of that "Buffalo Truck Driver" group. Man, what great times we all had together.

At the end of the AFL's existence, Wayne and Jim were voted to the All-Time AFL team as starters. Jim was a center and Wayne was a guard. That alone says what Wayne's peers felt and thought about him.

LESTER HAYES

As cornerback Willie Brown's career was winding down, along came Lester Hayes in 1977. Lester was a unique person and an incredible talent.

Two original Raiders, Wayne Hawkins (65) and me at Frank Youell Field in 1965. *Photo courtesy of Tom Flores.*

He had tremendously quick feet. I don't know if I have ever seen any feet that were quicker. His feet could move at a pace that seemed like 100 miles per hour.

He played kind of a monster position, or almost a linebacker position, at Texas A&M. He had a lot of Aggie jokes. He was constantly talking, some of it probably due to nerves. We could see right off the bat that Lester was going to be a good football player. We didn't know how good at the time, but we found out later. He turned out to be one of the best.

Lester had all of the abilities: size, quick feet, and explosion. Lester was similar to Willie, although Willie was a little smoother. Lester was more of a rat-a-tat-tat type of guy when he backed up. The one thing people have to realize about Lester is that he was a very bright football player. He studied. He took film home all the time. I'm not sure if they ever got out of the trunk of his car, but I do know that he studied enough. It was obvious on Sundays. He knew what the opposing player was going to do. Many times, we wondered if he was guessing, but he wasn't; he was reading the routes and he knew what to expect.

He had a phenomenal year in 1980. He intercepted 13 passes, which is still a Raiders season record. That was our Super Bowl year as a wild card.

Lester became a starter early in his career, his second year I think, and he stayed there all the way until his career was over in 1986.

My Car Broke Down . . . Again

Lester was notorious for being right on time, down to the last second. He always cut it close. I remember one time he was late because his car broke down. I said to him, "You have a $55,000 car that breaks down every week. That's kind of hard to imagine." He just looked at me and said, "Coach, I can't talk right now; I've got to get to your meeting." What could I say? He was late, and I fined him for it. I thought maybe instead of a $55,000 car, he should have gotten a $75,000 car that wouldn't break down or get a flat tire, or whatever the excuses were.

Textbook Cornerback

There are some qualities that cornerbacks in the National Football League must have to succeed: they have to be fearless, proud, and tenacious. They are alone out there, with 65,000 people watching to see who wins that battle. And a defensive back is going to get beat once in a while. There is not a corner alive who hasn't been beaten for a touchdown. You have to win most of the battles, though, to be successful. Lester won most of them, just as Willie won most of his. That's why we won Super Bowls—we always had

Lester Hayes, shown here playing in the AFC Championship Game in January 1984, was an incredible cornerback for the Raiders. *Photo courtesy of the Oakland Raiders.*

great corners, going back to the early 1960s. Lester certainly fit the criteria for a cornerback.

A team has to have good corners if it's going to play an aggressive style of defense. The Raiders have always drafted good corners and tried to get the good corners from other teams.

When Lester and Seattle's Steve Largent would go head-to-head, it was quite a battle. Both of them were very aggressive and very competitive. Steve would run immaculate routes and Lester tried to read what Steve was going to do next. That made for some great battles on Sundays.

I still see Lester every once in a while. He is living in the San Joaquin Valley. He decided to stay in California. I think he's living around Modesto, occasionally making appearances and doing card signings. He looks good. I don't know if he can still back-peddle, but he looks like he might be able to.

MIKE HAYNES

Mike Haynes, in my opinion, is the best corner with whom I ever have been associated. He was the complete package. Mike was not drafted by the Raiders, nor did he make his initial mark with the Raiders. He started with New England as its number-one draft choice, the fifth pick overall, in 1976.

Mike is what you look for in a corner. He had size, about 6-foot-2 and about 185 to 190 pounds. He was lean and well-built, and he could fly. He ran with such ease. He could run with the best receivers and he had the height, so if they were running side by side, a quarterback had to throw over him. He also had great jumping ability and body control.

Early in Mike's career, he was an incredible return man on special teams for the Patriots. He ran back two punts for touchdowns during his rookie season. When he left New England, he was the team's all-time punt return leader with 1,159 yards. He could return punts like a Pro Bowler, which he became in a very short time.

If you needed a training film on how to play the corner, Mike should be the one to make it. His incredible play at corner is why he was inducted into the Hall of Fame in 1997. That's how he helped us win many games, including a Super Bowl.

Last-Minute Trade

Mike joined the Raiders in 1983. We were into the season and we had a good football team, there's no question. We were on the verge of being great. Lester was playing one corner, and Ted Watts was the other corner that we had drafted. Ted probably would have been better suited as safety, but we had him at a corner. The trade deadline was running down. Mike was looking to get out of New England, and they were looking to move him.

As things turned out—and it seems the Raiders are notorious for this—the deal came right down to the deadline. The agreement was made, but then the deadline passed and there was some confusion as to whether the trade was going to be allowed. Mike was in our building with his agent when the chaos ensued. However, as it often was in the National Football League, and especially with the Raiders, the league accommodated the trade, and Mike became a Raider.

As Good As It Gets

We did not acquire Mike so that he could be a backup, so almost immediately after he joined the team he became a starter for us. With Lester Hayes on one side and Mike on the other, we could do some things that were just incredible. Vann McElroy was our free safety. Mike Davis was a strong safety. With the addition of Mike, Ted Watts became one of our nickelbacks. We had so much talent back there. Every one of them could run.

Mike was the epitome of what coaches look for in a defensive corner. He had size, height, speed, agility, and intelligence. Our Pro Bowl players were all intelligent football players. A few of them maybe were not so bright off the field and some of them got in trouble every once in a while, but they were all bright football players. They made quick and wise decisions and prepared themselves well for games.

Of all the corners who ever played this game, Mike stands tall in my mind. I love Willie Brown and I love Lester, but Mike stands tall. That trio was as good as it gets!

TED HENDRICKS

Ted Hendricks, in my opinion, was the most dominating defensive player I have ever coached. I played with and coached some great defensive players—Hall of Fame players—but Ted was the most dominating.

Ted was such a unique guy when he came out of college. He was nicknamed "The Stork" because he was so tall and gangly. Some of the scouts did not know exactly where he was going to play. Some were reluctant to even look at him for their team because they felt he was too tall and awkward to play linebacker and too skinny to be a defensive end. Obviously, he ended up at linebacker, but I think he could have played either position.

Ted had great leverage for a guy who stood 6-foot-7 or -8. He had great power and vision; he could see over almost anybody who was trying to block him. When the ball carrier got close, Ted would just throw his opponent aside. The scouting report on Ted that I got from some other teams was "don't piss him off, because then he becomes a real terror." He was a great player as it was, but he became an awesome player when he was angry.

Mike Hayes was the complete package as a cornerback. *Photo courtesy of the Oakland Raiders.*

Ted was a very bright person. He would get bored by the time defensive day was done, so he watched us go through the offense. By the time Friday arrived, he knew exactly what everybody was doing on both sides of the ball.

Ted was an interesting guy. During practice he would create diversions for himself, and we would have to tell him to go away and stand somewhere else. It was almost like giving a kid a timeout—"Go over there and stand while we finish the practice." Oh, he was a pain in the ass sometimes. I almost had to chuckle to myself because he was that way.

He was also a prankster. One year during training camp, he had so much energy that when most guys were lying in bed between practices he was walking around the facility. He would cut jokes out of the newspaper and put them on the bulletin board in my office or on my door if it pertained to some kind of torture that we might be putting on him.

Is That One of the Four Horsemen?
No, It's Just Ted Hendricks

One time, when John Madden was coaching, we went to one of the local schools to practice because our fields were pretty well torn up and we were going to practice late in the afternoon. Everybody was out on the field except John and some of the coaches. John usually was the last one to the field, which meant when he came out it was time to start. On this particular day he came out and all the guys were standing around, staring. We could tell that something was about to happen, but we didn't know what. John blew the whistle to get started, but nobody did anything.

All of a sudden, way in the distance, a guy on a horse wearing complete football gear and carrying a lance came charging in as if he was Sir Lancelot or somebody. Actually, it was Ted. That cracked everybody up. It was hilarious. Even John almost cracked up. He didn't know what to do. As coaches, what could we do? We couldn't get mad at Ted, because he wasn't trying to screw up practice. He was just trying to keep it light, which is something he always tried to do. That's the way he was. We finally got practice going and actually had a good one. Ted just had to do something to make it fun.

One time during a game on *Monday Night Football* during the week of Halloween, Ted was wearing a Halloween mask. I'm surprised he didn't go onto the field with the mask on.

On the field, though, he was tremendously competitive. I saw him at the end of his career, playing in so much pain that it hurt me to watch him. If he was at the game, he wasn't about to sit down. Still, he gave us a good half before I made him sit down.

A New Nickname

Ted's nickname, "The Stork," disappeared when he was with the Raiders. They actually called him "Kick 'em in the Head Ted." I think it all came from the time that he had accidentally nudged some guy's headgear with his foot. They ran it repeatedly in the films. I'm not exactly sure how the whole thing came about, but I do know that out of that came the new nickname.

His Raiders teammates called him Kick 'em in the Head Ted and people from way back called him The Stork. I just called him a great football player. Ted—No. 83, Hall of Famer, bright, intelligent, a pain in the ass sometimes, but an outstanding person and a very bright guy. He's now living in Chicago and is still a great Raiders fan—a true legend.

BO JACKSON

Bo Jackson was a different type of player than Marcus Allen, one of his backfield mates. Bo had incredible speed for a 230-pounder. He was Cliff Branch-type fast, but weighing 60 pounds more. At the time, he probably was the fastest man on our team. It was amazing to watch him. He had an

extra gear that most players don't have. He could outrun defenders to the perimeter and then kick it into that other gear. I only had him for part of the year. Because of his baseball commitments I didn't have him for training camp or the first part of the season. When you don't have a guy like that in training camp, it's tough to know what you're going to do with him. I didn't really have a plan for him because I was so involved with the season.

Playing Catch-Up

Tampa Bay drafted Bo in the first round in 1986, but the Buccaneers were so bad that he didn't sign with them. He sat out that season, becoming eligible for the 1987 draft. Since he had already started his baseball career with the Kansas City Royals and because of what happened with Tampa, many teams passed on Bo. In fact, he was still sitting there in the seventh round, so we took him. We figured that if he were interested in playing football, we would be interested in him. Once baseball season was over, which was well into our season, Bo joined the team. Obviously, he had cram sessions trying to catch up with everyone and learning what he had to do. It was not long, though, before everybody realized what great ability this guy had.

Bo's First Practice

The first time I saw Bo run in practice was incredible. He'd run inside, but he loved to bounce to the outside and run in the open field. He loved to run. We all loved to watch him. In fact, when we first saw him, several of the players and coaches could only exclaim, "Oh!" as if they were watching a fireworks display. In many ways, that was what we were watching. It was hard to imagine that a guy as big as Bo could have that kind of speed and

Ted Hendricks (83) was a dominating defensive player. *Photo courtesy of the Oakland Raiders.*

explosiveness. In that first practice, there was one play where he ran to the left and then all of a sudden he hit that other gear and just took off.

Competition

The biggest question when Bo came was how we were going to get Marcus and Bo equal time or enough time. We were concerned with how it was going to affect Marcus, our star and featured back since 1982. Could we utilize them both? Would there be enough room for both of them?

We did not bring Bo in to sit on the bench, but on the other hand, there's a pecking order at times in professional sports. Bo was used to being the premier guy at Auburn, but Marcus was used to being the premier guy with the Raiders.

I'm sure Marcus didn't like some of the things we were doing, but he adjusted well. We had a formation that included both Marcus and Bo at the same time. In that situation, Marcus was the fullback and Bo was the halfback. If we could have had that tandem in training camp, we would have had all sorts of options during the season. That would have been impressive.

We played Bo out wide as a receiver, forcing defenses to play off him. The first game we did that, we threw him a deep slant that resulted in a touchdown. The defender, which was the strong safety, was 20 yards off him. The idea was to throw him a quick hitch pass and make the other team tackle him, which was a chore. We did some great things with him, but we simply ran out of time to do more.

Bye-Bye, Boz

Bo showed the nation what he could do during a *Monday Night Football* game in Seattle. One play was a 93-yard touchdown run. He ran to the left side and then took off. Several Seahawks had angles on him, but they couldn't catch him. His attitude was that if he had room, nobody was going to catch him. One of the Seahawks with an angle was Kenny Easley, who was an incredibly fast person. Bo just shifted and then shifted again and ran through the end zone and out the tunnel. I think he stopped in Tacoma or some place. The whole Kingdome was buzzing.

The guy who blocked for him on that play was Marcus. We had them both in the backfield at the same time.

I think the play that most people remember from that game was Bo "running over" Brian Bosworth. The fans raved that of all people, he ran over the "Boz," but he would have run over anybody to get to the end zone. We were on about the four-yard line, and Bo went wide to the left. There he was—Brian Bosworth. Bo lowered his shoulder, and Brian hit him at about the three-yard line. Bo just bowled him over into the end zone. It seems like everybody went crazy when that happened and the network kept showing the replay.

People were down on Brian because of the multicolored hair and all that stuff, but Bo would have run over whoever was out there. It didn't matter. He was an incredible force in the open. Boz had Bo wrapped up, but Bo took him into the end zone before going down because of his incredible power.

All-Around Athlete

In terms of overall athletic ability, I don't think there was any sport that Bo couldn't master. The one thing that was so impressive about Bo was his attitude. He had such a positive attitude. There was no question in his mind that he could do something and do it well. He took a lot of pride in that. He was an amazing guy.

This One's For You, Coach

In 1989, when I was with the Seattle Seahawks as their president and general manager, the Royals were playing in Seattle against the Mariners. Bo was

playing for the Royals. I grabbed our PR guy, Gary Wright, and said, "Let's go to the game." We went down onto the field before the game to see Bo.

George Brett, who also was with the Royals, came over to talk to me. I've known George and his brothers for a long time because they were from El Segundo, which is where we used to have our training facility. He mentioned that Bo was his roommate, so we started talking about him. He told me that Bo was incredible as a baseball player, especially his speed to first base. He also had a powerful arm.

Bo came over and picked me up with a huge bear hug. We chatted for a minute, but then he had some things to do to get ready for the game. I told him that we couldn't stay long, so if he was going to do something spectacular, to do it early in the game. We laughed about it.

However, in the first inning Bo went up to the plate and—*BOOM!*— launched a hit nearly to the third deck in left field. As he circled the bases, I told Gary that we could go. Whether you believe it or not, as far as I'm concerned, Bo did that for me.

Family Man

In my opinion, Bo could have been one of the top five backs ever. He was already a great running back, but consistency is what you look for. After his rookie season, 1987, I retired from the Raiders and eventually he had that unfortunate hip injury.

Guys like Bo come around so rarely. It's very sad that his career ended so quickly. I don't know who to compare him with other than Jim Thorpe, who could do it all. Bo could do it all.

Off the field, Bo was a very nice person. He was a quiet family man. He was very protective of his wife and kids.

It would have been amazing to see what a healthy Bo Jackson could have done in a full career. *Photo courtesy of the Oakland Raiders.*

He made some great commercials and was in a couple of episodes of different TV shows. He is a good businessman and one of the great role models in the history of the sport. He wasn't a big loudmouth. It would have been fun to coach him for a whole career. It probably would have been like coaching Marcus, which was like driving a Mercedes.

TOM KEATING

We got Tom Keating from Buffalo in 1966. Although he wasn't big, he was a very quick and powerful defensive lineman. He was very bright and explosive. He lifted weights and had tremendous power and leverage for his size.

Al Davis traded for Tom, and he immediately became a starter for us. He was part of the Super Bowl II team that played the Packers in Miami. I was not on that team; I had already been traded.

But Tom and I became very good friends. We buddied around together often. He loved to hear and tell stories. He had a great laugh.

He loved hearing all the history about the league and about the characters—and believe me, we had many characters. He enjoyed everything about the game and everything about the Raiders.

Cerveza, Señor

Tom's running mate became Ben Davidson. The big thing they had in common was a passion for motorcycles. They would travel the country in the off-season. They would just get on their bikes and head across the country. One year, they went into Mexico. Here are these two big guys, just driving along. They certainly didn't look like Hell's Angels; they looked like two big guys traveling around the country.

It's funny to picture, though, because Ben is bilingual. Heck, he knows Spanish better than I do. That helped him when he and Tom went on their motorcycle trips. Here are these two big guys, Ben at 6-foot-7 and Tom at 6-foot-4, going across country on motorcycles. Imagine them pulling into some little pueblo in Mexico. Here's this "gringo," with a handlebar mustache, speaking fluent Spanish in a raspy voice. The Mexican people had to be astounded by him. Ben is such a personable guy, though, that I bet it didn't take long before he was drinking one of their beers and sharing tortillas and beans with them.

Tom always was interested in history and geographical history around the country. Tom had a mission. He knew where he was going. He knew what he wanted to do. Now he is living in Washington, D.C., actually working for a living. Knowing Tom and his penchant for stories, he's probably schmoozing with all the diplomats.

DARYLE LAMONICA

I had been with the Raiders since their first day of existence, and we went through some bleak years. We started getting better in 1963, and in 1965, you could see that the team was about to be a true contender in the American Football League.

Suddenly, in 1967, the Raiders made a huge trade. They acquired quarterback Daryle Lamonica, a former Notre Dame standout, from Buffalo for some quarterback named Tom Flores—yep, me. That probably was the beginning of the end for me because I got hurt both years in Buffalo, even though I ended up in Kansas City for a Super Bowl win.

That was the beginning for Daryle, and what a tremendous beginning. He came into a team that was ripe and ready to win with talented players. The team went 13-1 that year. Daryle won about every honor there was to win—MVP in the league, the All-Star Game—and then he played in Super Bowl II against the Green Bay Packers.

Even though the Raiders lost the Super Bowl, it still was quite an accomplishment for Daryle, who, at that point, had matured. He was ready to

perform in the system. The way the system was set up was perfect for Daryle. Most teams at that time were playing man-to-man defense. There weren't many three-deep or two-deep zones in those days. Daryle had a potent offense with Fred Biletnikoff, Warren Wells, Bill Miller, and Billy Cannon. Those people could get up the field. Daryle just picked apart defenses, primarily with the deep ball. That's how he acquired the term the "Mad Bomber," and that he was. He loved to throw the ball deep. He had a magnificent arm and could throw deep and with accuracy down the field. Daryle made a mark in the American Football League and the NFL after the merger.

When I came back as an assistant coach in 1972, Daryle's career was starting to wind down. That year, Kenny Stabler was Daryle's backup. Daryle had some problems along the way, so John Madden started using Kenny more in the fourth quarter. In 1972, Kenny won the starting job, but then he had some problems, so Daryle replaced him during the early season and started the rest of the year.

In 1973, the permanent switch finally was made.

Daryle was a valley boy from Clovis, California. He probably picked in many of the same vineyards that I picked or in some of the same peach orchards. We had similar backgrounds, except he was from Clovis, which in those days was a hick town. If someone wanted to get into a fight, all he had to do was go to Clovis. It was that kind of town. Really!

They had the Clovis Rodeo every year, and if you went there as an "outsider," you usually got into a little scuffle. Keep in mind, though, fights in those days were a little different from today's fights. They are certainly much worse today.

Overall, Daryle was in a perfect atmosphere for growing up because he loved to hunt and fish. After Daryle's career ended, he returned to his roots.

Daryle Lamonica talks with head coach John Madden during a timeout in 1969. *Photo courtesy of the Oakland Raiders.*

He's living in Clovis and doing what a lot of us do: playing golf, enjoying life, and telling old stories, which get better all the time.

Daryle has some great stories to tell because he had a marvelous career.

HOWIE LONG

We drafted Howie Long in the second round out of Villanova in 1981. When we drafted him, I think he had just turned 21 years old. He was a young pup. I remember watching him on films before the 1981 draft, and here was this guy running all over the field. He was running from sideline to sideline. His team didn't play in a great league, but it had some good competition. Watching him on film was funny, because he'd be lined up at defensive end and the ball would go away from him, so he'd chase it all the way across the field. Then he'd chase it back, rush the passer, and run back down the field when the pass was thrown. We couldn't help but notice him. He was all over the place! Even though he was going hard on every play, we thought, "Wow! What is he supposed to be doing?" We really didn't know what his assignment was.

Howie caught the eye of our defensive line coach, Earl Leggett, and, obviously, the eye of Al Davis. Most combines, or scouting networks—which rated players by rounds—rated Howie somewhere around the fourth or fifth round. Holding true to form, we had our own rating system and we took him in the second round. Another great second-rounder!

Howie was no exception to our second-round-pick rule. In his case, however, he had several things going for him. He was young and he had great size, speed, incredible upper-body power, and a lot of power in his lower body—his thighs and lower legs. He had tremendous leverage, and that helped him later when he developed the "rip move," which was one of the best.

But he was green as grass. Green as grass! When he was in training camp during his rookie season, he was, once again, running all over the place. We weren't exactly sure where he was going all the time, but he worked hard.

Howie made himself a great player because he was serious about football. He studied it, and he worked hard at it. If anybody ever refined himself into a Pro Bowl-caliber player, Howie was the guy. He was the textbook example of how a player should work and study.

In fact, the night before every game, he and a group of defensive linemen, along with safety Vann McElroy, would all gather in one of their rooms—usually Howie's room. After we were done with the quarterback meeting we would send the projector into their room and they would watch tape until bed check. When game time came, Howie was prepared.

What a great career for this young guy from the projects and from a small college with Ma—his grandmother—watching from above. I'm sure she is very proud of him. I know I am. He was the epitome of a Hall of Fame player and person.

Ah, Ma!

Howie came from an interesting background, because his grandmother raised him in the projects in Boston. His parents were estranged and divorced. And I am not so sure how close he was to them. (Although I met his father at the Hall of Fame induction in Canton in 2000.)

The only name by which I knew his grandmother was "Ma," which is what Howie called her.

One night during training camp in Howie's rookie season, one of my assistants came in and said, "Coach, there is a 'Ma' on the phone." I thought to myself, "Howie's Ma?" So I took the call. It had to be late back in Boston because it certainly was late on the West Coast. This nice, soft voice said, "I'm Howie's grandma."

"Ah, Ma, how are you doing?"

She told me she was fine and then said, "I just called to see to how my Howie is doing." (I had to smile.)

I said, "Howie is doing fine. He's working hard, he's learning, and we're very pleased with him. We're very happy to have him here."

She said, "Well, I just want to make sure that he is being a good boy, behaving and taking care of himself."

I said, "I assure you, Ma, he is being good and we will take good care of him because we think a lot of him."

When I told Howie the next day that "Ma" had called, he turned about 25 shades of red. But it was kind of a nice, warm, fuzzy feeling that I had and hopefully he shared.

I got to meet her eventually when we played back in Boston, and she came to the game. Quite a remarkable gal! She did a heck of a job raising that young kid.

Ma passed away a few years ago, but she was special.

ROD MARTIN

Rod Martin was one of the great linebackers for the Raiders. He was a skinny guy, weighing about 190 pounds, when he came out of USC in 1977. He could run like a deer. We drafted him in the 12th round that year. That was a good draft for us. We also drafted Mike Davis, Lester Hayes, and Jeff Barnes. We already had Phil Villapiano and Ted Hendricks, so by getting Rod late in the draft, he could develop and we weren't using a high draft pick.

Rod was an interesting story. We had him playing special teams and then we'd cut him. We'd bring him back and then cut him. Bring him back—well, you get the picture. We could make constant roster moves like those with

---

Hard work paid off for Howie Long, seen here in Oakland on the day of his ring ceremony, as he became a Hall of Farner. *Photo courtesy of Tom Flores.*

Rod, since we didn't have any fear of anyone picking him up because he wasn't rated very high.

In 1980, we traded Phil to Buffalo for Bobby Chandler, and Rod became a starter for us. Ted was on the left side where he belonged and Rod was on the right side. That tandem was outstanding. By that time, Rod had grown up. He had tremendously strong hands. If he put his hands on you, you were history. He had great power in his legs, he could run, he was very bright, and he had a million-dollar smile.

The epitome of his young career was in Super Bowl XV in New Orleans, when he intercepted three passes. In my opinion, he was the defensive player of the game without question. He had a good career with the Raiders, until he retired in 1988.

Rod is a classy guy. Off the field, at home, he's a pussycat with his wife and two lovely daughters. He has no chance with the three of them. It's funny because here's a macho guy who played a macho sport, but he goes home and he's a pussycat because those girls know how to say "Hi, Daddy."

JOHN MATUSZAK

John Matuszak, who joined the Raiders in 1976, was one of the biggest guys I had ever seen. "The Tooz" was about 6-foot-7, weighed 310 pounds, had tremendous coordination, and was a great dancer. It's hard to imagine that a guy that big would be able to dance like he could.

John, out of Tampa University, was a No. 1 draft choice of the Kansas City Chiefs. There was always a question mark as to whether anybody could handle him. He was kind of a wild and crazy guy, and he didn't disappoint anybody as far as being wild and crazy. He just did a lot of stupid things off the field. On the field he was a force, but did any team want to put up with the aggravation of his antics off the field? Well, he didn't last very long in Kansas City. I think he went to Washington for about one day. Obviously, he didn't last there very long. In 1976, we lost three defensive linemen in training camp and were faced with a big personnel problem. So, in true Raider form, we signed John.

I remember confronting him once when I was an assistant coach. We were about to get on an airplane out of Houston. I grabbed him and took him aside because he was doing something that he probably shouldn't have been doing. He wasn't a bad guy and he wasn't arrogant, he just didn't have much of a concern with what he was doing. He asked me why he couldn't do certain things, like drink. To be honest, in those days there wasn't the testing that there is today, but if there had been he probably would have been suspended.

We went to a three-man line that year, with John and Otis Sistrunk as the two defensive ends. It was an awesome front seven. Our defense was loaded. John didn't know how to play the three-man line; we just went to it because the linebackers were our best people. We had more linebackers than defensive linemen, and John gave us strength at that position.

We went 13-1 in the regular season that year. With the exception of losing to New England, we went right through the league and then through the playoffs. We got revenge when we beat New England in the first playoff game and then beat Pittsburgh in the championship game to go to Super Bowl XI in Pasadena, where we handily beat the Minnesota Vikings.

John was a force, but he was always on the edge. I'm sure John Madden had some conversations with him, but I remember that when I became head coach we had to talk. I had him in my office one time after he did something wrong. There I was, 6-foot-1, looking up at this big monster, pointing my finger, just as you might do with your kids. I said, "John, you have got to behave." I went on telling him that he had to do this and he had to do that. He had his head down and he said, "I'm sorry, Coach. I won't do it again. I'm sorry. I apologize. I'll behave." It was almost as if I should have put him in the corner facing the wall and told him he was in timeout. When he left the room I had to chuckle, because I had reprimanded this giant of a man.

The Tooz was the kind of guy who, if you ordered a cocktail, he would have a triple. If you had one thing, he had to have three of them. It was because he was The Tooz.

Eventually, all of that wore his body out, and he died way too young. There will never be anybody like him. He's one of the most memorable Raiders of all time—The Tooz!

KENT McCLOUGHAN

Kent McCloughan, out of the University of Nebraska, came to the Raiders in 1965. He was a young cornerback and played in a man-to-man scheme most of the time. Boy, he could run like a deer. In fact, he was a state track champion in Nebraska.

During Kent's rookie season, we were playing a preseason game at San Diego when the Chargers had John Hadl at quarterback and Lance Alworth at receiver. Kent was a little star-struck with Lance. Kent was about 6-foot-1, 185 pounds, and he was covering Lance, a future Hall of Famer, man-to-man. That much pressure was enough to make a rookie throw up in the locker room. I don't know if Kent threw up, because I was not sitting next to him, but I do know he was nervous!

During the game, John threw a pass to Lance and Kent picked it off. He ran it back for a touchdown. How's that for the young rookie defending against a Hall of Famer? How's that for the way to start your rookie year?

Kent was fearless. He just lined up, played tight coverage all the way, and was able to run with just about any receiver. He had five great years with the Raiders. It was a short career because of an injury, but it was a good career.

John Matuszak (72) had incredible size and power for a linebacker. *Photo courtesy of the Oakland Raiders.*

During his time playing, though, he was a two-time All-AFL player and played in Super Bowl II.

Kent has been with the Raiders since 1972 as a scout. One of his sons, David, who went to the University of Colorado and played in the NFL, likewise is a scout with the Raiders. Another of his three sons, Scott, is a scout with the Seattle Seahawks. Football is a family affair for the McCloughans. David and his wife, Elnora, did a nice job raising their sons. They are a neat family.

VANN McELROY

A guy who never really got as many of the accolades as he deserved is Vann McElroy, whom the Raiders drafted in the third round in 1982 out of Baylor. Vann was an outstanding safety. He was a tough, tenacious guy from Uvalde, Texas.

Vann was incredibly nice and polite off the field. I think his father was a Baptist minister. On the field, though, Vann turned into a vicious safety. On Saturday nights before a game, he always went to the room with the defensive linemen, led by Howie Long, to talk about or watch film of Sunday's opponent.

I still see Vann occasionally. He has a wonderful wife, Gail, and beautiful children. I actually talked with him while working on this book. It's nice to rehash some of the memories. Vann was a very bright guy and one of the unsung heroes of the Silver and Black. Besides that, anybody from a little town called Uvalde, Texas, can't be all that bad.

MATT MILLEN

The Raiders drafted Matt Millen in the second round in 1980. He was a defensive tackle from Penn State. They had two tackles who were like bookends—not very tall, but thick. Matt was all over the place. He had great leverage and lateral pursuit, and we felt that he could stand up and play inside in a two-point stance. When we got Matt, we were playing a three-man line. With the three-man line, the inside backers are playing against guards most of the time.

We didn't waste much time putting Matt in with the first team. But there was some frustration in his life. He was such a competitive and serious-minded guy about football. As we found out later, he just loved the game. He loved practices and playing the game and he worked hard.

During his rookie year, we were running a goal-line drill where we were throwing play-action passes. The same guy kept getting open in the end zone. That player happened to be Matt's guy. Matt was mad! He was screaming, "What's wrong? Why can't I cover? What's going on? What am I doing wrong?"

I calmly looked at him and said, "If you just quiet down, Matt, we will tell you what you're doing wrong."

He looked at me and said, "Oh, OK." That was it. We showed him and then he realized what he was doing wrong. We never had to repeat directions more than once or twice because he would get things pretty quickly. He was a fast learner.

The same thing happened once during a game. He came off the field yelling, "I'm playing terrible; I stink. Why am I playing so terrible?" I got in his face and said, "I don't know why you're playing terrible, but find out and get it right." All he had to do was calm down a little bit because he was so emotional.

Hard Worker

Talk about a gym rat, though. Matt loved everything about football and everything surrounding it. One night I came out of my office in Los Angeles to get some fresh air—it was about 8:00—and there was Matt, working out in the weight room. I asked him what he was doing.

"Aw, I got bored at home, so I thought I'd come down and lift some weights," he said.

If we'd had two-a-days during the regular season, he probably would have been happy because he would have taken part in every drill. On special teams day, he was on the opposition. On the offense's day, he was on the opposing team. He would do it all, and he would be there from early in the morning until late at night. He just had a passion for the game.

As Good as It Gets

At the end of Matt's rookie year, we won Super Bowl XV. He came to me and said, "Coach, I guess that's it."

"What are you talking about?"

He said, "Well, rookie . . . Super Bowl . . . what's left?" I kind of laughed—and I still laugh when I think about this story—and said, "Maybe we can do this again, don't you think?"

Sure enough, we did it again, three years later in Tampa.

Just the Shirt on His Back

One time when we were traveling, I asked the guys not to dress shabby. I told them, "If you're going to wear jeans, make sure they're designer jeans and that you wear a nice, pressed shirt."

So Matt wore a plaid shirt and jeans and carried a toothbrush and his game plan. That was it. He said, "I travel light, Coach."

Everywhere a Winner

After Matt left the Raiders following the 1988 season, all he did was help the 49ers win a Super Bowl. He then went to the Redskins and helped them win a Super Bowl. In fact, he's the only player to win a Super Bowl

Matt Millen was one of the hardest working players I coached. *Photo courtesy of the Oakland Raiders.*

with three teams. So I guess you'd have to say that Matt Millen has had a very successful career as a football player and as an announcer. Now that he's in management, I hope he'll do well. Who knows how he'll do, but Matt loves challenges and hopefully he will win in this next part of his dream.

JIM OTTO

I think every football fan knows the name Jim Otto. He is one of the greatest centers of all time and one of the most remarkable stories in the history of professional football. The injuries that he sustained while he was playing and the aftermath, all the different things that he's had to do, and all the surgeries he had to go through after his playing years—28 knee operations, two artificial shoulders, and a rod up his spine—make him an incredible story. He has faced death on at least one occasion. Talk about a walking miracle.

There was a period of time a few years ago when he had a staph infection in one of his artificial knees. They had to remove the knee, and he was without a knee for a few months while he recovered from the staph infection. He was at home, and his wife, Sally, had to apply the intravenous flow of antibiotics.

Jim is just a remarkable guy. Every time you think he's down, he gets right back up.

Mr. Raider

Jim and I started playing together in 1960. He was another of the original Raiders. He is one of the few guys in the league who spent his entire professional career with one football team. He went through as a player and then joined the front office when he retired in 1974. He is a very successful businessman, owning Burger Kings in the Sacramento and Auburn areas. He still maintains his relationship with the Raiders in some capacity, and to this day, he even has an office with the Raiders. He does some community events and organizing for some of the Raiders programs.

Without Jim, it just wouldn't seem like the Raiders. If you want to call someone Mr. Oakland Raider, Jim would be the guy to whom you would have to give that label.

Standard Bearer

When Jim was a rookie out of Miami University in 1960 he was an undersized lineman. He came to camp thinking that he was going to be a linebacker. He was 217 pounds, which wasn't big for an offensive lineman. But wisely and fortunately, the coaches moved him to offensive center in a very short time—within a day I think.

Jim always could snap the ball in deep snaps. He could zip the ball on point-after-touchdown attempts, long snaps, and punts. He always had a tremendous pop to his snaps. Jim was just a tough guy. He lined up and played every down. He grew into the center position and became one of the all-time greatest. He certainly was the best center to play in the AFL from 1960-69.

Jim was so tough that when he played, he could play hurt. He had a huge helmet. He would put that head right into the defender's chest and pop him. Jim loved contact. He loved playing the game, and he loved practicing the game. He did all of it so well that he set the standard for many years to come. He was *the* man. He definitely set the standard for centers in the Oakland Raiders organization.

Family Man

Jim married Sally, a girl he knew from the University of Miami. He adopted Jennifer, Sally's daughter from a previous marriage, and then they adopted their son, Jimmy.

Jim was a fun person to be around. We used to drink beer together and laugh and tell stories. The stories always got better as the years went on, obviously.

Where Am I?

Jim, through the years, would get banged up because he was always hitting somebody and they were usually bigger than he was. Jim would be so dinged that sometimes he didn't even know where he was. We would just prop him up in the huddle, I'd call a play, and Jim's cobwebs would clear by

Some of the Raiders through the years: (from left) Jeff George, Jim Plunkett, Daryle Lamonica, Jim Otto, and me. *Photo courtesy of Tom Flores.*

the time he went to the line of scrimmage. He was always ready for the next play. Well, maybe he wasn't exactly ready, but he would always snap the ball on the cadence and then bop somebody before you would know it—he was back to being Jim Otto.

Actions Speak Louder Than Words

Jim learned a lesson early in his career about saying too much to the media. We were going to play the San Diego Chargers in 1961, and they had a guy named Ernie Ladd, who was a huge rookie. He was about 6-foot-9, 315 pounds, but he wasn't fat—he was massive. He was one of the biggest guys I'd ever seen in my life. Jim made a statement during the week that we were going to kick his butt one way or another.

When we lined up that Sunday at Candlestick Park, the first thing I noticed was that Ernie wasn't lined up in his normal spot—he was lined up right on Jim. When the battle began, I think Ernie's only concern was that he would knock Jim back a few times and make him eat his words. Jim battled him and battled him all game long and took more hits than usual.

After that day, if Jim wanted to knock somebody's head off, he wouldn't talk about it; he would just go ahead and do it. And, believe me, he knocked off a lot of heads and knocked a lot of people back. He was just a superb player.

One Last Hit

When I came back to Oakland in 1972 as an assistant coach, Jim had already played a long time. He still was playing well, but his knees sometimes got so bad that he could hardly play any more. He was just hobbling around the field.

We were playing a preseason game—I don't remember the opponent— and it was time for Jim to step down and retire. All he wanted to do was get one last pop—one last good hit. So John Madden put him in the game.

He went into the game, snapped the ball, and just nailed somebody. I don't know who it was, but it was a pop to remember. He just nailed the guy on about a leg and a half that he had to use. And then he came hobbling off the field with a huge smile on his face. He didn't have the blood that usually ran down his face during the course of a game, but he was laughing, whooping, and smiling because he got his last hit. He knew that was going to be the last hit of his career, and he wanted to make it a good one. Believe me, it was.

He left the game the way he started—by lining up, snapping the ball, and just nailing somebody. That was classic Jim.

JIM PLUNKETT

Like many NFL teams, the Raiders can be identified by their quarterbacks through the decades. This current decade, at least the first part of it, belongs to Rich Gannon. Tom Flores was the early 1960s, and Daryle Lamonica was the late 1960s. Kenny Stabler was the 1970s. And Jim Plunkett was the 1980s. Actually, it may be more accurate to say that eventually the 1980s belonged to Jim.

Jim and I had—and still have—a great relationship. As long as I've known him, he has always been a very honest, straightforward guy.

The only thing Jim did as a player was win. He won the Heisman Trophy in 1970. He won the NFL's Rookie of the Year award with Boston. And he won two Super Bowls with the Raiders, including the Super Bowl XV MVP award. I will never understand why he's not in the Pro Football Hall of Fame yet.

Early in the 1978 season, the 49ers released Jim. It wasn't a shock, because when we saw him that preseason, I thought his arm was shot. He was not throwing very well. So Ron Wolf wanted to work him out. I'm not so sure John Madden was for us working out Jim, because we had Kenny Stabler as our starter and David Humm as the backup. Usually you don't want to upset anybody or create any unnecessary chaos. (I'm not sure too many things could have affected Kenny, though.)

I worked Jim out in front of John, Ron, and Al Davis on the players' day off. I wanted to know if he could still throw and if he still had the arm strength. He had some surgeries on his throwing arm, which affected him in San Francisco. We had played against him that year in a preseason game in San Francisco, and he didn't look like the same guy I remembered.

So Jim threw the ball and threw it well. He made all the throws that were necessary; he moved around with that lumbering type of movement that he had. He was very powerful and strong. I didn't think there was anything wrong and obviously neither did the bosses, because we signed him and made him third string behind Kenny and David. For that first year, 1978, we wanted mainly for Jim to learn the system and get his confidence back.

In 1979 when I became the Raiders' head coach, Jim went through regular training camp with us. By that time he understood the system. He learned it by sitting and watching without pressure. He was being reborn. He actually had a better camp than Kenny did, but Kenny was the incumbent and our leader. Jim was a good backup because of his experience and his ability.

We ended 9-7 that season, one game out of the playoffs. Despite all kinds of injuries, we managed to stay competitive.

In 1980, we traded Kenny for Dan Pastorini. I was not in favor of the trade, but I went along with it. It probably was time for Kenny to go, but we could have traded him for a first-round draft choice. However, since we traded a starter for a starter, Jim was still second string. In hindsight, he should have been the starter.

We started the season 2-2, going into a home game against Kansas City. The Chiefs beat us badly that day, 31-17. Dan was out with a broken leg. There were all kinds of rumors that I was to be fired. It was kind of ugly for a while. (Fortunately, it was just a rumor.) All of a sudden, Jim was our guy. We played at home the next week, and we beat San Diego.

Even though we were 3-3, we were trying to find our way above water going into Pittsburgh the following week for a Monday night game in front of the whole country. Jim had a marvelous game that night. All the guys were making big plays. We won 45-34.

I still remember that the plane ride home after the game was just incredible. I had the flu, with the chills and everything, but I still felt great on the flight home. When West Coast teams play Monday night on the East Coast, they get home at about 5 or 6 a.m. on Tuesday morning. As head coach I couldn't take off much time because I had to be back at the office in two or three hours, getting ready for next Sunday's game.

It's amazing that we all didn't get pneumonia. Had we lost, I probably would have gotten pneumonia. Luckily, we won.

Chunky Plunkett

Jim was well-liked by his teammates. Gene Upshaw used to give everybody a nickname. They called Jim "Chunky." Most people called him "Plunk," but the players called him Chunky in the huddle because he was fighting his weight that entire season.

Unfortunately, he pulled a muscle and couldn't jog. He used to love to jog. In fact, he ran in a marathon once. I don't know how or why, but he did. He had puffed up a little bit by the end of the 1980 season, and by the time we got to the Super Bowl, Jim was a little heavier than he wanted to be. But he was just an amazing warrior. He helped us win that Super Bowl, and he was named the MVP.

Mature Quarterback

Jim was probably the last quarterback for the Raiders who called his own plays. When Jim went down to an injury and then backup Marc Wilson

---

Jim Plunkett (16) had a lumbering way about him. He gets a block here from Mark van Eeghen (30) in a game against Kansas City. *Photo courtesy of Tom Flores.*

went down, we called every play for Rusty Hilger. We realized that we were asking guys coming out of college, who had never called a play in their lives, to play the game at the highest level and call their own plays for the first time. It hit us that that probably wasn't the greatest plan. So we started calling all the plays all the time.

When Jim got well, he had a tough time with the adjustment. Eventually he got it, but it drove him crazy. I told him that if he had a play that he wanted to run, to signal us, and we wouldn't send in our play. He had a tremendous feel for the game.

I sent in a play one time on third down and he didn't call it. We didn't pick up the first down. When he came off the field, I asked him what happened to the play I called. He said he didn't think we were ready for it. Thinking about it, he was right. I think I called for it out of desperation.

100-Percent Champion

Throughout his career, Jim took a beating because of the way he played. He was big and not a real nimble guy, so when he ran with the ball or when he was in the pocket, he took some pretty good hits. He was such a courageous guy, though. He didn't avoid the contact when he knew that he was going to be hit, and he delivered the ball. But in 1983, he was really beat up. We were doing OK. We were holding our own and were in first place. Still, Jim was beat up and struggling a little bit.

We took a 5-1 record to Seattle in October. We lost, 38-36, committing seven turnovers. We seemed to cough it up all day. We were minus-13 in turnovers that year, which is just incredible. By the end of that Seattle game, Jim was really beat up. He wasn't the type of quarterback who could avoid a hit, because he was so big.

The Players

The next week at Dallas we made a change, starting Marc at quarterback. Jim wasn't happy about it, but he went along with it. I don't blame him for being ticked off. Who's going to be happy about being demoted? Nevertheless, Marc had a great night against the Cowboys. We won in the last minute of the game. We lost the next week to Seattle at home in the L.A. Coliseum. Then we went to Kansas City.

We were playing a typically close game against the Chiefs. There seemed to be a jillion people in Arrowhead Stadium—all wearing red. All of a sudden, Marc went down. He came out, and we got Jim ready to play. I asked Marc if he was OK. He said, "Coach, if you want to win this game, you better put Jim in, because I think I'm hurt pretty bad." He was right. His broken shoulder kept him out for the rest of the season.

So there we were again—time for our team's savior, Jim Plunkett. It was almost like he came in on a white horse. He came into the game against the Chiefs, and he was incredible. He was like a new person. He had spring to his legs, he was bouncing and was as agile as I had ever seen him. He had life in his arm. He obviously had healed from the beating that he took prior to us sitting him down. He was flawless that game and nearly flawless the rest of the season.

The rest is history.

Once again, Jim took us all the way to Super Bowl XVIII in Tampa, where we beat the Washington Redskins. Jim had a big night, making some big plays. Jim was a big-play guy. He played great in big games and was a champion through and through.

It's interesting that two times during Jim's career he became the starter because of the starter's injuries, and he led us to the Super Bowl both times.

It's funny to think back to the end of training camp in 1980, when Jim came to me wanting to be released or traded. I am extremely thankful that Jim decided to stay. I would bet he's thankful that things worked out the way that they did. I thank God for Jim Plunkett.

ART POWELL

Art Powell, in my opinion, was one of the greatest receivers in the history of the American Football League. He probably was one of the first of what I would call prototypes that could play today.

I first met Art on the field during college in 1957, when I was playing for the College of the Pacific. He was a wide receiver at San Jose State, about 6-foot-3 and 185 pounds. In those days, we played both ways—offense and defense. When we were on defense, I was the cornerback guarding Art. Saying I was going to *guard* Art is a misnomer, or at least an exaggeration. Luckily, we played a zone defense. On one particular play, Art was running a pass route, and he slipped and fell. The ball hit me right in the chest. I couldn't help but intercept it, so to this day, my claim to fame with Art is that I covered him and intercepted a pass off him. Of course, I don't usually go into the particulars of how it happened. I just say that it did happen.

Prototype Receiver

Art left San Jose State after his sophomore year. He went up to Canada, and he played there in 1958 and I think 1959. In those days, unless a player had some kind of hardship, he was not allowed to play in the National Football League until he had been out of high school for four years. When Art came back from Canada, he played for the Philadelphia Eagles for a short time, and then, in 1960, he joined the New York Titans (who became the Jets in 1963). Art instantly became a big hit.

Art was their featured receiver, and he was outstanding. We only saw him twice a year, so we didn't really get a chance to realize how good a receiver he was or how he was maturing into a great receiver. The Eagles tried him primarily as a defensive back. He played with the Titans from 1960-62 and in 1963 he became a free agent. Al Davis signed him.

I hadn't really seen Art since that game in college, but his talent was immediately obvious. Al had Art running patterns with certain types of moves and with certain types of releases. He could do it all.

Art would have been great in any era. He would have been great today because he was what teams today look for in a wide receiver. Besides being built like a tight end, he was strong and had great hands. He had terrific concentration and he could go deep or catch the short ball. He had deceptive speed because of his long stride.

Art established himself as one of the all-time best receivers in Raiders history. His 16 touchdowns in 1963 still ranks second on the all-time list, two behind Marcus Allen and tied with Pete Banaszak. The remarkable thing about Art's 16, however, is that we were playing only 14 games in a season back then.

Charlie Powell

Art's older brother, Charlie Powell, preceded him with the Raiders. Charlie was one of the original Raiders, playing in 1960 and 1961 as a defensive end. He joined the San Francisco 49ers right out of high school because he had a hardship.

He was a pro boxer during the off-season. At one point, he tried to become a full-time pro boxer. He actually fought some big-name guys.

Charlie was a fun-loving, happy-go-lucky guy. Art was more on the serious side. Both of them were very talented, but they were different types of players with different personalities.

Go-To Guy

Art was my favorite receiver. We were playing the Bills late in the 1964 season at Frank Youell Field. We were trailing in the fourth quarter, 13-9. We had one play left in the game, and, obviously, we needed a touchdown.

We were on about the four-yard line. The one guy we wanted to go to in that situation was Art. I called his play and then threw the ball high, knowing that he could go up even though he was playing against one of the better corners in the league, Butch Bird. Art went up, and he caught the ball. The place went crazy. All 18,000 people were screaming and yelling; many of them rushed the field in celebration.

Art will go down as one of the great Raiders wide receivers. The great players want the ball with one play or one series left. Art was that kind of player. He wanted the ball, and he knew he could make that play every time.

ART SHELL

One thing about the Raiders is that very few guys have come in and started right off the bat. Usually, guys have people that could play ahead of them, so there was no urgency to rush. The Raiders drafted Art Shell in the third round of the 1968 draft. When he came in, he was a guard, but they were grooming him to become the left tackle.

When he finally became the starting left tackle in 1970 or 1971, he was there forever.

We never let the linemen get big. We kept Art under 300 pounds, or at least for Thursday night weigh-ins after practice he was less than 300 pounds. By game time, he probably would be right at 300 pounds. Art always fought his weight, but he worked hard to maintain it. He had the best feet of any guy that I ever had seen of that size. He would glide. His feet were almost like those of a ballet dancer.

Art was the epitome of a left tackle, because he was intelligent, nimble, explosive, quick, and quiet. He never even said "boo." You never knew if he was in the huddle or in the meeting rooms because he was so quiet. However, I'll say this: When Art said something, people listened, because it was always something profound.

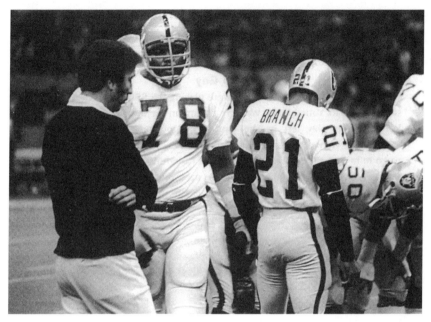

Art Shell (78), Cliff Branch, and others go through pregame drills. *Photo courtesy of Tom Flores.*

Gene Upshaw and Art were roommates. Those were two of the best.

Art helped us win two Super Bowls, XI and XV, and then he became a coach for me on my staff when he retired from playing after the 1982 season. He became an assistant line coach with Sam Boghosian. He had the same quiet demeanor, but he cared about the players. He took a lot of notes.

Minority Coach

All of Art's work paid off for him, because in 1989, he became the first black head coach in the National Football League. A "cute" thing happened when he was hired as head coach. In an interview he was asked, "How does it feel to be the first minority head coach in professional football?" He said,

"I wasn't the first minority coach." The reporter gave him a quizzical look. Then Art said, "Tom Flores was the first minority coach; I'm the second."

I thought it was neat that he said that, especially since he was right. Last time I checked, Hispanics, Mexicans, Chicanos, or whatever we are this week, are minorities. We seem to be changing titles all the time, but we're still Americans and we're still descendents from Mexico. I'm very proud of that fact in my career. Art made me even more proud with his statement.

MIKE SIANI

If the stories in this chapter weren't in alphabetical order, I'd put Mike Siani with Cliff Branch. Mike was the first-round pick in 1972 out of Villanova, the same year we picked Cliff in the fourth round. After I spent that week with Cliff in Colorado, I spent the next week with Mike at Villanova, because he was involved in baseball. At one point, there were a lot of questions as to whether he would be signing a Major League Baseball contract or an NFL contract.

Mike Siani was a 6-foot-2, 190-pound wide receiver with excellent feet and hands, not tremendous speed, but enough speed that he could get deep at times. He was big, strong, and very competitive. During that week at Villanova after baseball practice on a couple of days, he'd go through the rookie book, and we would go to the other diamond and he would run some routes in his baseball cleats. I would walk him through, he would run some, and then I would throw him the ball.

A Career Cut Short

In 1972, the starting wide receivers for the regular-season opener at Pittsburgh were Cliff and Fred Biletnikoff. Kenny Stabler was the starting quarterback. Early in the game, Kenny threw a ball that bounced off Cliff's chest for an interception. Cliff dropped a few other passes that should have been caught, and Kenny missed some of his targets. Neither Cliff nor Kenny were having a good start.

So Daryle Lamonica went in and replaced Kenny, and Mike replaced Cliff. Daryle and Mike connected immediately in the second half. Mike caught two long passes for touchdowns against the two-deep zone. Daryle threw them both perfectly. We lost the game, 34-28, but from that game on, Daryle and Mike remained starters.

Mike went on to have a very productive rookie year. He was a starter until 1974, when he ruptured his Achilles tendon. He stayed with us through our first winning Super Bowl, XI in 1976, and played one more season after that. It was unfortunate that Mike had that Achilles problem because that slowed him down. I think it shortened his career. He was the type of receiver, without injury, who could have played a long time even if he wasn't a starter, because he was so productive and he could catch the ball inside the red zone.

Mike was very good because of his abilities to jump and dive and make acrobatic catches. However, because of the Achilles injury, he had to slow down. Any time you lose half a step when you're not a burner to begin with, your career is shortened. He remains one of the most productive wide receivers in the history of the Raiders.

KENNY "THE SNAKE" STABLER

Many people don't know this, but even though Kenny "The Snake" Stabler came in as a rookie in 1968, he didn't make the Raiders squad until 1970. He actually played for a minor-league team. Then he did not start until his fifth year in pro ball. He replaced Daryle Lamonica.

The NFL defenses had changed and zone defenses were coming into vogue. The two-deep zone and three-deep zone suited Snake perfectly. He could pick apart any defense if he had time. He ate up zone defenses.

Snake had an extremely quick delivery. He threw three-quarters some-times or side-arm. He didn't have a tremendously strong arm, but he was accurate and he had the luxury of playing with some great receivers—guys like Cliff Branch, Fred Biletnikoff, Mike Siani, Raymond Chester, and David Casper. Kenny took full advantage of all of them.

He knew, for instance, that Cliff was so fast that he had to throw the ball hard and throw it quickly. Otherwise, Cliff would get out of his reach. Sometimes he threw the ball so hard that he'd spin himself completely around almost as if he were a discus thrower.

The remarkable thing about Snake was that he was just as good on Wednesday afternoon, Thursday afternoon, Friday, and Monday as he was on Sunday. I don't think he ever got riled. He was just a happy-go-lucky guy all week. He was a fun guy, but he was competitive as hell.

Sometimes, if things weren't going well in the passing game during prac-tice, we'd leave him alone and let him work his way out of it. After getting frustrated, he'd get that look in his eye, which many of the great players get. He'd have snot coming out of his nose and down from his beard, and we knew to leave him alone. He would find some way to work himself out of a jam even if it wasn't something we wanted him to do.

He might get pissed off, but he never got riled. He'd find ways to com-plete passes and to move the ball and get the offense going again. That was just his nature. He was one of the best in the two-minute drill because of his ability to make quick decisions and deliver the ball quickly.

Hiss, Hiss

Kenny came from Alabama, which is where he got his nickname, "The Snake." At one time, before his knees were beaten up, he was a great runner. He was a great scrambler and runner, with good speed. In fact, during the "Immaculate Reception" game, against Pittsburgh, he ran about 50 yards,

Kenny "The Snake" Stabler was one of the best Raiders quarterbacks ever.
Photo courtesy of the Oakland Raiders.

including 40 yards for a touchdown that put us ahead. We thought that was enough to win the game until that stupid play at the end of the game where Franco Harris picked that ball that bounced off Frenchy Fuqua and ran all the way for the touchdown.

Nevertheless, Snake could maneuver like that. People say that he used to move around like a snake. It wasn't because he hissed or anything.

Pet Name

Kenny used to tell me stories about playing for Bear Bryant at Alabama. He admired Bear tremendously. If you played for Bear once, you were a Bear guy all the way. It was like playing for Woody Hayes. If you liked Woody at all, you loved him forever. If you didn't like him, you wouldn't even talk about him. Bear was the same kind of guy.

Kenny said that Bear called everybody the same thing. He called everybody a "turd." Evidently, that was an endearing term from the Bear toward his players.

General Snake

Kenny was the kind of guy who would have made a great general, because the other players craved his leadership. They would follow him anywhere and everywhere. They would follow him into battle, which they did. You could see the fire in his eyes, spit coming out of his mouth, and his beard all wet from perspiration. He'd do that sometimes in practice just to get the juices flowing because things weren't going his way. Kenny lived hard off the field, played hard on the field, and was very well-liked by people around him. He certainly was one of the most popular men ever to play for the Silver and Black.

JACK TATUM

Jack Tatum, No. 32, from New Jersey. That's how most opponents would like to remember him. However, they usually remember him as the "Assassin."

Jack was an intelligent guy and was such an articulate speaker, yet he could be in a room and you wouldn't even know he was around. If someone did overlook him, he would scare the heck out of them because he had that look in his eyes.

On the field, Jack was the most devastating hitter that I've ever seen. He had so much power. And his power was not delivered just while he was leaning over; he could be just as powerful standing straight up. There weren't many guys who liked to come over the middle when Jack was there as a safety. That's what happened in those days, though, when we played a three-deep zone or man-to-man coverage. The offense had better know who was in the middle of the field before they went that direction, if Jack was anywhere close. Nowadays, teams throw in the middle randomly. I think that's because a lot of guys got hurt and some guys were fined because of it, but Jack was not a dirty player.

As I said, Jack was very intelligent. Coming out of high school, he could have gone anywhere in the country. He ended up at Ohio State and played for Woody Hayes. He was one of "Woody's guys." It's easy to see why he would fall into that group. Jack was tougher than nails, and there was no way any coach or player was going to intimidate him out of a program.

Woody was notorious for intimidation, almost like a marine drill sergeant. If a player survived it, he became a great Buckeye and a Woody fan. Jack certainly was a Woody fan. Jack used to enjoy reminiscing, and we all had great laughs when Jack told some of his favorite Woody stories.

Show No Emotion

Jack was a fierce competitor; however, he was very quiet, never said too many words, and never celebrated after he made a tackle. Jumping up and down because he mauled some guy was not enjoyable for Jack. Tackling guys was what he was supposed to do. His job was to make tackles, punish people, and then get up and go back to the huddle.

I think the most emotion we ever saw out of him was when he stood up and looked at someone on the ground. For example, in Super Bowl XI when he hit Sammy White, he just looked down at Sammy as he lay there and then he hustled back to the defensive huddle. There weren't any high-fives or running around making sure that everybody could see his number. That was considered "bush league," but we see it so much nowadays. Everybody seems to be doing it. No, Jack was from the old school—the hard-knock school.

He was one classy guy for the Raiders.

In 1980 when I was the head coach, we traded him to Houston, where he finished his career. His career had wound down, and I brought him in and talked to him about the situation. He simply said, "I understand. I know what you're doing, and I know why you're doing it."

He understood everything. He said all the right things. I felt so bad, but he actually made me feel better. I was supposed to make him feel good about being traded, and he ended up making me feel good instead. He lasted through one more year, and then he retired.

Jack lives in the Oakland area, and he works for the National Football League on game days. For home games, he's the guy who reports if the uniforms aren't being worn properly. Let it be known, that uniform better be worn properly. I wouldn't argue with Jack even today. If he says, "Put your pants up higher," I'd say, "Yes, sir."

"Pull down your socks."

"Yes, sir."

GENE UPSHAW

The Raiders drafted Gene Upshaw in the first round of the 1967 draft. By that time, I was playing in Buffalo. I didn't know who Gene was during his rookie season out of Texas A&M.

I later found out the Raiders mainly drafted Gene because they felt they needed somebody to block Buck Buchanan, the tremendous defensive tackle with the Kansas City Chiefs. I played with Buck—God rest his soul—for two years when I was with the Chiefs in 1969 and 1970. Buck was 6-foot-7, 270 pounds, and he could move. He had great ability, power, and closing speed. He literally could take over a ballgame if you didn't have someone to block him.

So the Raiders drafted Gene. As a rookie, Gene was probably 260-plus pounds, but he could run like a deer—and he loved to run. Whenever the

Raiders ran the sweep, Gene would run around there, setting the pace for the backs who were carrying the ball behind him.

You could always see Gene. He was always around the action and the pile. A bunch of players complained about Gene holding in those days. The referees would laugh about it. He may have held a little bit along with everybody else, but it was only illegal if you were caught. If you weren't caught, it wasn't illegal.

Gene was a very bright and loquacious guy. He never stopped talking. He talked in the huddle and talked on the sideline. He loved to talk. He gave everybody nicknames. He was voted the team captain and was a good leader because he kept the guys on the right track, especially in the locker room. He was certainly respected by his teammates and coaches.

Gene helped the Raiders reach three Super Bowls (II, XI, and XV), of which we won two. He played in six Pro Bowls and one AFL All-Star Game. He had a tremendous career on the field. He was inducted into the Hall of Fame in 1987.

Gene was also a Players Association representative and later became president of the Players Association. When you talk about leading the Players Association, you're talking about millions and millions of dollars to work with.

Gene used his influence to help some of the old-timers. The organization is doing some good things. There is a lot of money yet to be divided up and there are still a lot of things that can be done, but it is impossible to do it overnight.

Gene was self-educated in many ways, such as with speed-reading. He knew what he wanted, and he had a direction. I don't know if he knew exactly where he was going to end up, but he knew that he wanted to be something more than just an ex-football player. He certainly has reached that goal.

He was an outstanding football player, an outstanding person, and very successful. He had a tremendous memory for stories. There are all kinds of stories that we could tell, but unfortunately, many of them couldn't be published.

Gene was a good guy. He was proof that if you work and polish yourself off the field as well as on the field and you lead a good life, good things can happen. Indeed, good things happened for Gene.

MARK van EEGHEN

Thinking about some of the team's unsung heroes, Mark van Eeghen comes to mind immediately. Mark, a fullback, was drafted in the third round of the 1974 draft out of Colgate. Mark was a much-underrated player in my opinion. He was a great team guy—a lot better than people gave him credit for—with tremendous quickness and explosion as a rookie.

Marv Hubbard's career was starting to wind down, so we thought we would go back and tap the same well where we got Marv. The Colgate connection paid off. Immediately, Mark impressed us with his explosion, short bursts, and quickness, even though he was as nervous as a cat.

Mark threw up before every ballgame. In fact, between Mark and Fred Biletnikoff, we didn't know who threw up the most. It became a superstition that if one or both of them didn't throw up, we would not leave the locker room. That's the way it was. And they never let us down. To this day, I bet that if Mark has to go out and do something important, he probably throws up. That's just his nature.

Mark was one of our stars in the 1976 season. He had a Pro Bowl year. In Super Bowl XI, all the statistics went to Clarence Davis, but the guy who led the way for him, other than the offensive line, was Mark. Mark made the blocks on the weak backer or kicked out at the strong backer to free Clarence.

The Raiders drafted Gene Upshaw (63) largely because of his blocking ability. *Photo courtesy of the Oakland Raiders.*

Mark was equally as important during my first Super Bowl as a head coach, XV. He had a great year in 1980, but he also did the little things that were never noticed. He wasn't making the 60-yard run or the 60-yard completion, but he'd catch a little dink pass and pick up a first down. Or he would pick up a block and then make a tough run for a first down.

During our final drive against San Diego in the AFC Championship Game, Mark was one of the key players. After Jim Plunkett ran a couple times, lumbering down the field for a first down, he threw a short pass to Mark who picked up our first down. We held the ball for eight minutes, 30 seconds because of his key third-down plays.

Today, Mark lives in Rhode Island, and he still supports the Silver and Black. In my opinion, Mark was one of the greatest unsung heroes in the history of the Raiders.

PHIL VILLAPIANO

Phil Villapiano was an undersized linebacker for us from 1971-79, but he was a tough guy who could run well. I don't know if he would even qualify to be a strong-side linebacker today, but he was as tough as nails. He went to four Pro Bowls from 1973-76. He was already with the Raiders when I arrived in 1972 as an assistant coach.

Phil was ornery on and off the field. On it, he would just as soon smack you in the face or the mouth as anything else. He became known as a tough, wild, and crazy guy.

Phil is fun off the field. I remember one time when I was coach and he got into a little hassle with some of the Hell's Angels. It didn't turn out too well for Phil, but he survived. He was the spark plug of the team. He was always full of life—always a positive type of guy. He and John Matuszak hung out together when The Tooz joined the team. Phil was very well-liked on and off the field. The girls liked him a lot, because he was a good-looking guy.

Taking It for the Team

As Phil's career was winding down after the 1979 season, we had a chance to get Bobby Chandler, a wide receiver. We brought Bobby in for a workout, and he looked great. He was what we needed. We felt Bobby would really jump-start our offense and complement Cliff Branch. Before we made the trade, though, Al Davis called Phil. He asked, "How are you doing, Phil?"

Phil replied, "I'm doing fine. What's going on?"

"We're just working here, trying to get better," Al told him. "What do you think of Bobby Chandler?"

Phil was fired up. "He's wonderful. He's great. I love him. We got to go get him. What do they want for him?"

Al replied, "Well, Phil, they want you."

"No, no, don't do that. Don't do that!"

Well, we made the deal anyway. He was not suited up for the Bills the first time we played them since the trade because he was hurt. He was still a Raider in our hearts and in his. Despite the trade, Phil always was and always will be an Oakland Raider.

5

SUPER BOWL EXCELLENCE

During the Raiders' proud history, they have developed an excellence not shared with many other NFL teams. The Raiders have played in five Super Bowls—II, XI, XV, XVIII, and XXXVII winning three. Tom Flores was directly involved with each of those three championship teams. He was an assistant under John Madden in Super Bowl XI at the end of the 1976 season, and he was the head coach for Super Bowls XV and XVIII, after the 1980 and 1983 seasons, respectively. Incidentally, Tom was the first of only two men to be involved with winning Super Bowl teams as a player, an assistant coach, and a head coach. (The other is Mike Ditka.)

The following are some of Tom's most vivid memories of the Raiders' three winning Super Bowl teams.

SUPER BOWL XI

After avenging our only loss of the 1976 season to New England in the first round of the playoffs, we beat Pittsburgh and advanced to the Super Bowl. As we were getting ready for the Super Bowl, we had our game plan prepared, and everything was done. Head coach John Madden had OK'ed everything.

As he was directing practice on offensive day, with Kenny Stabler as the quarterback, it suddenly dawned on John that Kenny had not thrown an incompletion the entire practice or the entire offensive drill. John might have been the only one who realized that. Every ball had been caught. It was kind of an eerie thing because everything was just going way too well. It wasn't as if everybody was just standing around letting him make completions; the defense was working hard.

John had this look in his eye, and he blew the whistle. He said there was no need to go any farther because Snake couldn't get any sharper than he already was. That proved true, because on Super Bowl Sunday, Snake was outstanding, and so was the rest of the offense.

Predictions

As always the night before a game, we had our meeting with the quarterbacks and then the offensive coaches would discuss things after the players left. After Snake and his backup, David Humm, left, John asked nervously, "What do you think about it—tomorrow's game?"

Lew Erber jumped at the question and said, "Oh, I think it will be 40 to 6." John almost choked on his coffee. Even I choked a little. We were stunned that Lew thought it'd be such an outrageous score. I told them that I thought we'd win, but I didn't think it was going to be that lopsided. "I don't think there is any way these guys can beat us unless we screw it up or they do something on special teams," I continued.

John was a little nervous after that because we were a little too confident, I guess. However, any head coach probably would have been nervous after that. That's just the way head coaches are. I think deep down John was very

---

Championship trophies from Super Bowls XI, XV, and XVIII. *Photo courtesy of Tom Flores.*

positive about it too, but he couldn't let it show as much as the assistants could. A head coach has to be reserved.

The next day early in the game, wouldn't you know it, Ray Guy had a punt blocked. Ray rarely ever had a punt blocked. Nevertheless, the Vikings took over inside our five-yard line. I thought to myself, "Oh man, why did I say that last night? Me and my big, fat mouth!" I don't know if that was going through John's head, too, but it was going through mine.

Our defense made a tremendous goal-line stand, and the Vikings fumbled the ball. We recovered on our own two-yard line. From that point, we ran an off-tackle play to the left side and Clarence Davis got us out of there with about a 25-yard run. The rest is history. We dominated the game from then on, winning 32-14.

The Maverick

During the playoffs leading up to Super Bowl XI, the networks complained about actor James Garner, who is a huge Raiders fan, being on the field during our games. Of course, the network that was doing the Super Bowl that year, NBC, didn't mind him being on the sidelines, because he was on their network, but the league was on our tails.

Before Super Bowl XI, we were sitting in the back room of the locker room in Pasadena, and James came in. He said, laughing, "I've got three tickets, so they're going to have to kick me out of the game three times."

While he was in there talking to us, somebody was trying to get in the back door. James, who was close enough to us that it was almost as if he was part of the organization, opened the door to see who was there and what they wanted. James told the guy that he couldn't come in. The guy started pushing, and James pushed him right back. Finally, James grabbed him below the throat—of course, the guy's eyes got saucer big—and pushed him out. How about that! James Garner almost got in a rumble because some guy wanted to get in the Raiders locker room.

James locked the door, and I gave him my coach's coat and hat, because I was going to be upstairs in the booth anyway. I told him to turn up his collar and carry a football out there. By the time they noticed him, it'd be too late. So he did. As the game went on, we were doing so well that he took off the hat and coat. That's James. He loves the Raiders.

Sticky Situation

Fred Biletnikoff was the Most Valuable Player of the game. At that point in his career, he was into stickum pretty well.

Toward the end of the game, when it was pretty much in hand, we asked John if we could come out of the booth and down to the field. He said yes, so we all went down to share in the celebration.

I found Freddie and gave him a big hug. I almost couldn't get away from him with all of the stickum on his hands. Then Al Davis gave Fred a hug—same outcome. Al was covered with stickum—not as much as Fred, but he had quite a bit on him.

Fred had tears in his eyes, he was so happy. It was a great experience for me because of how far back we go and because he was down to his final couple of years as a player. It was incredible and our team's finest hour.

That was a big moment in John's coaching career. We all were happy because it was also a big moment in the Raiders' history. That was the organization's first Super Bowl victory, after losing Super Bowl II. This was a return to glory for the Raiders.

SUPER BOWL XV

We went to Super Bowl XV in New Orleans at the end of my second year as the head coach. We were the wild card that year. We beat Houston 27-7 in the wild card game. The Oilers had been favored that year to go to the Super Bowl. Then we went to Cleveland and beat them with the wind

The scene was set for us in Super Bowl XV in New Orleans. *Photo courtesy of Tom Flores.*

chill factor at 39 degrees below zero. Mike Davis intercepted a pass late in the game, helping us win that one.

Then we went to San Diego for the AFC Championship Game. The Raiders and the Chargers always had wild and crazy games there. Well, we beat them, 34-27, by holding on to the ball for more than eight minutes at the end of the game and not letting their offense get back on the field. As I was talking to Jim Plunkett, getting him ready for our final drive, Ted Hendricks came over and said to Jim, "Don't let them get the ball back, because we can't stop them."

I looked over my shoulder and said, "Get out of here. You're crazy." Then I went on with the instructions to Jim. He simply was marvelous on that drive.

After winning that game, we had two weeks to prepare for the Philadelphia Eagles and Super Bowl XV. Throughout the season and peaking during the playoffs, there was a feud between commissioner Pete Rozelle and Al Davis over the pending move from Oakland to Los Angeles. Particularly, they were sparring in the media about the rule that said an owner couldn't move his team.

Great—as I'm leading the Raiders to the Super Bowl for the first time as a head coach, that was going on and our "out of control" Raiders were about to face the great Dick Vermeil and his paramilitary-type team. To top it all off, guess what happened. I became sick on Monday, the very first night we were in town. I was up all night. I didn't have a solid thing to eat until Thursday night.

We had press day on Tuesday, and during the press conference I had a fever and was doing my best not to throw up. I just wanted to get back to my room, but I was required to spend a certain number of hours on the field talking to every press guy. And then we had practice at Tulane University.

Hi, My Name Is . . .

When I first sat down at the podium for the press conference, I actually introduced myself in front of a thousand writers and media, and then I just kept on going on my comments. I started by saying, "I'd like to introduce myself. I am the head coach." Of course, those reporters in that room had no sense of humor—nobody laughed. I thought, "Oh no, that bombed."

Later, one of the reporters from Oakland asked me why I introduced myself. I said, "I didn't know if you guys knew who I was or that I was actually involved in this football game." Everything in the papers and the electronic media talked about the great Dick Vermeil and Pete Rozelle versus Al Davis.

People kept asking me if I thought that if we won Al would accept the trophy from Pete. I kept saying, "Al Davis and, I believe, the commissioner, would never do anything to degrade this game. It would be handled with professionalism."

Looking back, it was handled just as I predicted.

If It Weren't for Bad Luck

After the press day on Tuesday, I had to get over to Tulane for a light practice and to finalize some of the things in the game plan. Fortunately, having the extra week between the conference championship and the Super Bowl allowed us to do most of our preparation in Oakland.

I went outside to get on one of our buses and discovered that both of them had left. They left! They left without me! I thought to myself, "This is not starting well. First, I had to introduce myself today to the press so they would at least know I'm coaching and involved in this game. Now, the buses have left me." I was furious, but also I just wanted to get back.

Two young players also missed the bus, so the three of us jumped in a cab. Well, the cab driver didn't know how to get to Tulane. We got lost!

When the driver got close to the facility I said, "There it is, over there." I paid him, and we walked across a muddy field. I was so pissed off, but I didn't have time to even point fingers at anybody because I had to get practice under way. I was also so sick that I didn't feel like making a big deal out of it, even though I knew who was responsible.

Later, once things had calmed down, I started laughing. I couldn't help it. I think everything that could have gone wrong that week, did. Not only did the press not know who I was, I evidently needed to introduce myself to some of my own organization. How's that for a humbling experience.

Curfew, Schmurfew

As I mentioned, we were seen as the big, bad, undisciplined Raiders—the wild and crazy guys. We had a team meeting Monday night, and I told the guys that we weren't going to have a curfew until Wednesday night. Gene Upshaw, Art Shell, and a couple of the other leaders stood up and said, "No, Coach. You better start having curfew Tuesday night." I wasn't going to argue with that, so we set a midnight curfew Tuesday through Friday and then 11:00 p.m. on Saturday.

I told them that curfew fines started at $1,000, even for being one minute late. The fine would go up from there, depending on the severity. I told them that even though we were in a party town, we were here for business and that we would party when it was all over.

Wednesday, four players were late and incurred a fine. However, they were late because they rode with the team doctor to the practice at Tulane University and the doctor got lost. So I did not fine them $1,000, only $500.

And then there was Wednesday night. Everybody was in on time and stayed in except for John Matuszak, who was missing in action. Now, if you're going to sneak out after curfew and you're 6-foot-7, 320 pounds, don't you think you're going to be recognized on Bourbon Street? Well, Matuz was there. Thursday it was written up in the papers as if the whole team was out on the town.

So Thursday, I brought him in to give me a reason. I told him that he was going to be fined regardless, but I wanted to know why. "What were you doing?" I asked him.

He said, "Coach, I have an excuse. I had to go out to make sure that everybody else was in." I had to turn away so he couldn't see me getting ready to laugh, because he seemed to be serious! I don't know if he was, but he sure sounded serious.

I said, "Get out of here, go to your meeting, and let's get on with this. This is a big game."

"Yeah, it is, Coach, and it won't happen again."

We had no curfew violations other than Matuz that one night. Of course, the papers wrote it up as if the whole team was out partying.

Dick and his paramilitary camp were all staying in. We were the undisciplined Raiders. We had only two other issues the rest of the week. I fined one player because he left his playbook sitting in the lobby and it was turned in to me. Then, we had a guy who was two minutes late to a meeting because he was out roaming the halls, so I fined him. That was it. Overall, we had a great week of practice.

Leave it to Matuz to help uphold the Raiders' image during Super Bowl week. God rest his soul.

Discipline

Our guys were loose that week, unlike Dick's tightly wound Eagles. We gave our players a little freedom but not very much. We tried to make the

Jim Plunkett (16), seen here in Super Bowl XVIII, was the MVP of Super Bowl XV. *Photo courtesy of the Oakland Raiders.*

atmosphere as if we were at home. When the game came, we were supposed to be the undisciplined ones. We were supposed to be the renegades. Well, we made no mistakes. The Eagles made all the mistakes. We blocked a field goal attempt, had three interceptions, and we just beat them—we beat them good.

So which was the disciplined team? Which was the more prepared team? Evidently, we were.

The Super Bowl XV MVP That Almost Wasn't

Jim Plunkett came to me in training camp in 1980 and asked me to trade or release him, since he knew he wasn't going to be the starter. We had just acquired Dan Pastorini. The Raiders traded starting quarterback Kenny Stabler for Dan, another starter.

Jim and I talked about it, and I told him that I didn't think getting rid of him would help our team. He said he didn't like my decision and he didn't agree with it, but he was going to live with it. He was professional about it, and as it worked out he led us to a win in Super Bowl XV that season and won the game's MVP award.

Thank you, Mr. President

Even though it was tradition for the coach of the winning team to talk with the president of the United States on the phone after the game, I was not able talk to president Ronald Reagan, because that was the same year the hostages in Iran were released. The president sent a message apologizing, saying he had other things he had to do. I understood completely.

That reminds me of one of the most awesome things I saw that week. The Louisiana Superdome had a huge yellow ribbon around its perimeter to honor the hostages. It was just so impressive to drive up to the Superdome and see this huge yellow ribbon.

SUPER BOWL XVIII

Super Bowl XVIII down in Tampa was a wild and crazy time. But this time, we were a great football team. We had just walked all over our opponents in the playoffs. We crushed Pittsburgh and then blew out Seattle.

During the season we changed quarterbacks from Jim to Marc Wilson. The change was necessary because Jim was worn out. Marc played well until he broke his shoulder in Kansas City. By that time, though, Jim was rested,

It was a relief to talk with Bryant Gumbel in the winners locker room after Super Bowl XV. *Photo courtesy of Tom Flores.*

and he came back as if he were a new person. He led us the rest of the way in marvelous fashion.

There weren't too many unique incidents. Our guys were very professional throughout the entire season. We had acquired Mike Haynes right after the start of the season, and he gave us another level. We were so good defensively with Mike and Lester Hayes at the corners, and Vann McElroy and Mike Davis at the safeties.

We had a team of All-Pros—guys who were not necessarily in the Pro Bowl that season, but either had been before or were ready to be. Vann, Mike, and Lester were Pro Bowl players, as were Rod Martin and Ted Hendricks. Howie Long became a Pro Bowl player. Lyle Alzado had played in Pro Bowls. Matt Millen played in a Pro Bowl. That was an incredible defense.

We just had a great football team.

A Man of Few Words

Before I talk about the Super Bowl, I need to tell a story from the AFC Championship Game. I used to tell our players to do their talking with their play on the field, not in the media. The worst time to have to talk to the media is after a big game, win or lose. If you lost, you're mad and dejected, and you don't want to talk to anyone. If you won, you're higher than a kite, and you might say something that you'll regret.

Before playing Seattle in the AFC Championship Game that year, we had lost to them twice during the season. We had something like 13 turnovers in those two games. One of their players, in the locker room after they beat Miami to play us, said that they'd kill us just as they did during the regular season. Our guys were furious.

Nobody said anything, but that quote was on the bulletin board in the players' locker room. Right before we went onto the field for the game, after we took our 30 seconds of silence—prayer for the guys who want to—Lyle got up and asked me if he could say something real quick before I gave my final talk.

181

He got up and gave as emotional a short speech as I've ever heard. He talked about the Seahawks' lack of respect for us and about the article and on and on. His eyes were on fire. Shoot, he scared me. When he was finished and turned it back over to me, I just said, "OK, let's go."

I was not a big-emotion kind of guy before a game, so there was no way I could top that. Our guys were so hyped that we kicked the Seahawks' tails that day.

If your team isn't worth a damn, that bulletin board material won't really help. It might matter for the first quarter, but then talent will take over. We were a great football team that year.

Just Get Out There and Play

My pregame talks were not very lengthy because all of that was taken care of during the week. Halftime talks were different, because we had to make adjustments and we had the feel of the game at that time.

Shortly before halftime of Super Bowl XVIII in Tampa, Jack Squirek intercepted a pass and ran it back for a touchdown, putting us up 21-3. That pretty much broke the Redskins' backs going into the locker room. Remember, halftime at the Super Bowl lasts forever. That is even truer for the players. At the beginning of the half, I had something I was going to say before the guys went back to the field. However, when the time had come to say it, I forgot what it was that I was going to say. Oh well. I told the guys that we had a good first half and that if we kept it up, in 30 minutes we'd be world champions. And we were.

Our guys didn't need much motivation at halftime that day. Besides Marcus Allen's great running, our cornerbacks did a great job. We put seven guys on the line of scrimmage to stop the Redskins' running game. Therefore, when they went to pass to the outside guys, we had our defensive backs, Mike and Lester, who just shut them down.

I meet the press at Super Bowl XVIII. *Photo courtesy of Tom Flores.*

Great Plays

One play that sticks out was by our tight end, Don Hasselback, who has two sons who play quarterback in the NFL. We had acquired him from New England that season. During the game against the Redskins, he blocked a point-after attempt. Obviously one point didn't make a huge difference, but any time you can make a play like that it gives your guys a little extra momentum and takes something away from your opponent.

The player of the day, though, was Marcus Allen, who had 191 yards rushing that game, which was a Super Bowl record at the time. We always had certain things that we felt we could do against Washington.

Marcus made one run that was as spectacular as his long touchdown run. It was a five-yard run for a touchdown. You don't appreciate it until you see it in slow motion. It was a power off-tackle play to the left where he made one quick move, but the hole wasn't there, so he made another quick move and then he went into the end zone sideways. We were stuffed on that play and most backs in that situation would try to twist and turn to get back to the line of scrimmage, but Marcus instinctively took off the other way. He made it look so effortless that you cannot really appreciate it until it's in slow motion.

We did have some big-play passes for Cliff Branch and Todd Christensen. The Redskins were a tough team to run against, but we felt that we could get certain things done. Obviously, Marcus was our feature back. He made such great decisions and great cuts, and our line was superb that day.

Washington had beaten us 37-35 earlier in that season in an incredible game at Washington. From that, we had a good feel for what they did and

Marcus Allen, Super Bowl XVIII MVP, had a tremendous game against the Redskins. *Photos courtesy of the Oakland Raiders.*

how they did it. We were very confident in what we were going to do, but I never thought it would be a blowout. I felt we could move the ball against them; I just didn't know if we could stop them from scoring. Because we stuffed the line, and we choked their game. They got frustrated because things they had been doing all year didn't work in the Super Bowl.

We didn't have any problems with Washington in the Super Bowl, winning 38-9. The Redskins scored a ton of points that season. In fact, they broke the scoring record, so I was hoping that we could hold them down. I was hoping that we could beat them, but there's no way I thought we'd beat them that badly. Holding them to nine points was incredible. We simply dominated the game.

An Emotional Time

We picked up Lyle in 1982, the season before Super Bowl XVIII. Obviously, that 1983 season was a magical one for our team and for Lyle. I will never forget—with about a minute left in the game, even though we were up big, I was not going to celebrate until the final whistle. However, as I walked down the sideline, I turned and looked, and there was Lyle. Tears were just rolling down his cheeks. We looked at each other, and he pumped his fist a little. That's all he could do. He couldn't talk; he was so emotional. I turned away; otherwise I would have been crying, too.

I had a flashback to training camp in 1982, when he was in my office and wanted to retire. Had he not been convinced to stay, he never would have experienced what he experienced that night, that week, that year when we were the Super Bowl champs. After that game, he could say he was a world champion.

Just Ask for Directions, Please

The only bizarre thing that happened to us while we were in Tampa came after the game, on the way to the team party. Our bus driver got lost and it took us almost an hour to reach our destination. I was on the last bus with some fans and family. Finally, the bus driver had to stop, at our request, and ask for directions—I don't know if he was a bitter Redskins fan or a worn-out Buccaneers fan. Regardless, by the time we got to the party it was going along pretty well. We still made it and somehow found a way to enjoy ourselves.

See You in March

After the game, I met with the coaches to discuss the upcoming weeks. The scouting combines were scheduled to start the next week in New Orleans. The plan was for the coaches to go to New Orleans from Tampa, while I flew to Los Angeles for a ceremony before meeting them in New Orleans. I could tell that my coaches were ready for a mutiny.

I told them, "I have to fly back to L.A. for a reception at City Hall, and then I'll meet you in New Orleans. After the combines, you study your players and when you're done with your position you can go back to El Segundo, write up your reports, leave them with Ron Wolf, and I'll see you guys on March first."

They just sat there. Suddenly, they realized what I said—I gave them off the whole month of February. I never saw those guys move so quickly. I guess they were afraid I might change my mind. We had been living in hotels and away from our families for a long time because we were still in the process of moving to Los Angeles from Oakland.

When I got back to the office after the combine, I told someone that I gave the coaches a month off. I was asked who was going to mind the store. Hmmm. Well, I guess the guy who gave them the month off had to mind the store. So after we became the world champs of professional football, I took a whopping four days off to go see my wife and daughter, who were still in the Bay Area, and my sons, who were in college by that time. Then I was back minding the store. I guess a head coach's work is never done.

Go Raiders!

I cannot describe the feeling of holding up the Super Bowl trophy in front of fans in Los Angeles after winning XVIII. There's nothing quite like it. *Photo courtesy of Tom Flores.*